Glencoe

Literature

Common Core State Standards Edition

Project Practice Book

Glencoe Literature extension projects for

- Common Core State Standards
- College and Career Readiness
- 21st Century Skills

COURSE 3

McGraw Hill Education

Bothell, WA • Chicago, IL • Columbus, OH • New York, NY

glencoe.com

 Education

Copyright © 2012 by The McGraw-Hill Companies, Inc.

Send all inquiries to:
McGraw-Hill Education
8787 Orion Place
Columbus, OH 43240

ISBN: 978-0-07-661402-8
MHID: 0-07-661402-6

Printed in the United States of America.

2 3 4 5 6 7 8 9 REL 15 14 13 12 11

Contents

Reading Lessons: Informational Text

Writing Workshops

Vocabulary

Grade 8 Common Core State Standards

Reading Lessons: Literature

The People Could Fly

Virginia Hamilton

Glencoe Literature, pages 91–99

RL.8.10 Before starting the lesson, read the following selection and complete the lesson activities in **Glencoe Literature**.

"The People Could Fly" (pages 91–99)

In this lesson you will analyze and discuss the folktale "The People Could Fly." You will then research the elements of a folktale in order to write your own folktale. You may also publish your folktale online. Through your participation in the discussion and your work on the project, you will practice the following standards:

RL.8.3 **Key Ideas and Details**

- Analyze how particular lines of dialogue or incidents in a story propel the action or provoke a decision.

- Analyze how particular lines of dialogue or incidents in a story reveal aspects of a character.

RL.8.4
RL.8.5 **Craft and Structure**

- Determine the meaning of words and phrases as they are used in a text, including figurative and connotative meanings.

- Analyze the impact of specific word choices on meaning and tone.

- Compare and contrast the structure of two or more texts and analyze how the differing structure of each text contributes to its meaning and style.

Group Discussion

Discussing literature within a small group can help you grow as a reader and as a member of a learning community. Together, you and other group members can arrive at a better understanding of a selection, its ideas and craft, and its connection to other works and areas of study.

PLAN

RL.8.1
W.8.9, a
W.8.10
L.8.1
L.8.2, c

To prepare for discussion, build your content knowledge by examining the selection in greater detail. On your own, write your answers to the questions that follow, using text evidence. Make inferences about the text as you need to. You may also write additional questions about the selection that you wish to discuss with your group. Your teacher may review your answers before the discussion, so be sure to use correct grammar, spelling, punctuation, and capitalization.

RL.8.3 | **Dialogue** Conversation between characters in a literary work is called **dialogue**. Dialogue can help propel the **plot,** or sequence of events, in a story.

1. Choose three important lines of dialogue in "The People Could Fly." Then explain how each line of dialogue moves along the action of the plot or forces a decision.

_____

_____

_____

_____

_____

_____

2. Find three incidents in the story that move along the action of the plot or force a decision. Describe each incident and the effect(s) it causes.

_____

_____

_____

_____

_____

_____

_____

_____

RL.8.3 | **Character** A **character** is an individual in a literary work. An author may reveal a character's personality through direct statements about the character as well as through the character's words and actions and what others think and say about the character.

3. Choose two characters from the story. Fill out the chart below to answer the following questions about each character.

- Find two pieces of dialogue that help you learn more about each character. How does the dialogue reveal the character's personality?

- Find two incidents in the plot that help you learn more about each character. What do you learn about the character from these incidents?

Character	Dialogue and what it reveals about character's personality	Incidents and what each reveals about character's personality
	1. 2.	1. 2.
	1. 2.	1. 2.

RL.8.4 L.8.5, a

Figurative Language Writers use **figurative language** for descriptive effect, often to express ideas indirectly. Simile and metaphor are two kinds of figurative language. In a **simile** the words *like* or *as* are used to compare seemingly unlike things. *(The room was as still as a winter pond.)* A **metaphor** implies the comparison without using *like* or *as. (Her sister's voice was a clanging bell, awakening her.)*

4. Find the descriptions of the Master and of Sarah when she begins to fly. Write the figurative language that describes each. Which is a simile and which is a metaphor? How do you know? What does each figure of speech tell you about the character?

   the Master: _____

   _____

   _____

   _____

   Sarah: _____

   _____

   _____

   _____

RL.8.4 L.8.5

Connotation and Denotation A word's **denotation** is its dictionary definition. Its **connotation** is made up of the thoughts and feelings associated with the word.

5. Look up the word *freedom* in a dictionary. Find a use of the word *freedom* in the folktale that reflects one of the dictionary definitions. Which definition does it best reflect? Now find a use of the word *freedom* in the folktale that reflects connotation. What is the connotation of *freedom* as it is used here? How does the author express that connotation?

   Denotation: _____

   _____

   Connotation: _____

   _____

   _____

RL.8.5 **Structure** A text's **structure** is the order or pattern a writer uses to present ideas. The structure can contribute to a text's meaning and style.

6. "The Oxcart" on pages 356–362 of *Glencoe Literature* is a **cautionary tale.** Cautionary tales have a cause-and-effect structure: people break society's rules or misbehave and are then punished for what they've done. How would you describe the plot structure of "The People Could Fly"? How does its plot structure compare to the structure of "The Oxcart"? How does the structure of each text contribute to the text's meaning?

_____

_____

_____

_____

_____

RL.8.5 **Style** An author's style is his or her choice and arrangement of words and sentences. Style often reveals tone, or attitude. A text's structure can contribute to the style an author uses.

7. Give some examples of the author's style in "The Oxcart" and "The People Could Fly." What tone do these examples express? How does each text's structure contribute to the style? Fill out the chart to answer the questions.

	Examples of Style	How Structure Affects Style
"The Oxcart"	Examples: Tone:	
"The People Could Fly"	Examples: Tone:	

ASSIGN

SL.8.1, a Meet with your literature group to plan your discussion. Each group member should become the expert on one or two of the questions on pages 4–7. Each expert will then guide the discussion on his or her question(s). List the group members and the question(s) that each will become the expert on in the chart below.

Group Member	Question(s) to Present

To become an expert on your question(s), spend some extra time thinking about your question(s) and consulting the text for relevant details. Building on your question(s), write down one or two discussion points or related questions for group members to consider as they explore text issues.

_____

_____

_____

_____

_____

DISCUSS

SL.8.1a–d
SL.8.4
L.8.1
L.8.3

Break into your assigned literature group to conduct your discussion. The expert on question 1 should begin by reading aloud the question and leading the discussion in response. Follow this process for each question until you have covered them all.

Remember that literature groups contain room for disagreement. Healthy debate can help all members push their understanding to a new level. Use your time wisely so that you are able to discuss all the questions sufficiently.

In your discussion, follow the guidelines below.

Group Discussion

Discussion Guidelines

- Come to discussions prepared. Be sure you have read the material and are ready to probe and reflect on ideas and evidence.

- Set and follow rules for cooperative and collaborative discussions and decision-making, defining individual roles as needed.

- Track progress toward goals and deadlines.

- Express your ideas clearly and with sound reasoning. Support important points with relevant evidence and well-chosen details from the text.

- Speak with formal English grammar and usage. Use precise words to communicate your ideas.

- Pronounce clearly, speak at the proper volume, and make eye contact with audience members.

- Listen carefully so that you are able to pose questions that connect the ideas of several speakers and respond to others' questions with relevant evidence, observations, and ideas.

- Think about each speaker's ideas and claims. Is the reasoning sound? Is there enough evidence? Is there information that is not relevant?

- Acknowledge new information, and, when appropriate, qualify or justify your own views on the basis of the new evidence.

At the end of your discussion, be prepared to share the insights you have gained with your class. On the lines below, briefly summarize the most interesting ideas or insights you heard or experienced during the discussion.

_____

_____

_____

_____

The People Could Fly
Virginia Hamilton

21st Century Skills Project **Folktale**

Now that you have analyzed and discussed the folktale in detail, you will have the opportunity to extend your thinking about it creatively by participating in a group project. Your assignment is to write and publish your own folktale. In carrying out this project, you will follow the steps below:

- Do research to learn more about folktales of a variety of cultures.
- Write a folktale based on what you have learned in your research.
- If resources allow, publish your folktale online and present it to your classmates and teacher.

PART 1 Research Folktales and Write a Folktale

Before you begin writing, research three folktales from different cultures. Use research tools such as library books and the Internet.

W.8.7 **Research Notes** Take notes about plots, themes, and characters in folktales. Use the chart below to record your findings. Look for similarities between the plots, characters, and themes.

	Folktale 1	Folktale 2	Folktale 3
Plots			
Characters			
Themes			

Organize Your Folktale After you've completed your research, use what you have learned to write a folktale with your group. Discuss the plots, characters, and themes of the stories you researched to help get ideas. On the lines below, organize the events of your group's folktale into parts. Use the elements of a plot, as detailed below, to help you organize your folktale. Once you have organized events and developments, write your folktale as a group.

Exposition: Introduction of the characters, setting, and situation.

_____

_____

_____

_____

Rising action: Complications to the story's **conflict,** or central problem.

_____

_____

_____

_____

Climax: The point of highest emotional pitch.

_____

_____

_____

_____

Falling action: The result of the climax.

_____

_____

_____

_____

Resolution: The final outcome.

_____

_____

_____

W.8.3
W.8.4

Write Your Folktale Once you have organized your events, begin writing your folktale below and continue on a separate sheet of paper. Include descriptive details. Also make use of dialogue and incidents that move the action forward and that reveal aspects of characters and provoke the characters to make decisions. Make sure that your writing is clear and coherent, and that the development, organization, and style are appropriate to your task, purpose, and audience.

Present Your Folktale If you are not completing Part 2 of this 21st Century Skills Project, your teacher may ask you to present your folktale as the final activity of the project. You may also be evaluated on your presentation. Write or type your folktale neatly and turn it in to your teacher.

_____

_____

_____

_____

_____

_____

_____

_____

_____

_____

_____

_____

_____

_____

_____

_____

_____

_____

21st Century Skills Project

PART 2 Publish Online

W.8.6 | After your group has finished Part 1 of this project, publish your folktale online. Choose important words or phrases from your folktale. Then create hyperlinks to photographs, illustrations, videos, or other texts that help explain the relationships between information and your ideas in your folktale. This will help your readers get a better understanding of the story. For example, if your folktale is modeled on themes, events, or characters from other works, you can link to online versions or pictures from those stories.

Before you publish your folktale, fill in the chart below to help you decide which images or other media you want to link to.

Words or Phrases in Folktale	Description of Link (to photos, illustrations, videos, or other texts)

21st Century Skills Project

With your group, answer the questions below to help plan the online publishing of your folktale.

1. Where should we publish our folktale—on the school Web site or on another site?

   _____

   _____

   _____

2. What do we need to do to create the hyperlinks? How should they look?

   _____

   _____

   _____

   _____

3. How many links should we use? Is it possible to include too many links? Explain.

   _____

   _____

   _____

   _____

4. List the members of your group and the tasks each person will complete. Some tasks will need the help of more than one person.

Name	Tasks

21st Century Skills Project

W.8.6 **Publish and Present** Publish your folktale on your chosen site. Using your chart as a guide, set words and phrases in your story as hyperlinks to link them to photos, illustrations, videos, or other texts. Then send the URL (the Web address found in your Web browser) of your site to your teacher and classmates, so they can read and view your work.

After you have published your folktale, answer the following questions.

1. Which links best explain the message of your folktale? Why?

_____

_____

_____

_____

_____

2. Which part of this project was the most enjoyable? Which part of this project was the most challenging? Explain.

_____

_____

_____

_____

_____

SL.8.1
SL.8.2 **Evaluate** As you read and view your classmates' work, take notes about the content and effectiveness of their online folktales. Answer the questions below to guide your evaluation. Then use your notes and your answers to the questions to participate in a class discussion about the project.

1. How well does the folktale convey its story and message? Explain.

_____

_____

_____

_____

_____

21st Century Skills Project

2. What purpose do the links serve? How do they contribute to the overall presentation? Explain.

_____

_____

_____

_____

_____

_____

3. How might the group improve the project?

_____

_____

_____

_____

_____

_____

21st Century Skills Project

The Drummer Boy of Shiloh

Ray Bradbury

Glencoe Literature, pages 310–319

RL.8.10 | Before starting the lesson, read the following selection and complete the lesson activities in ***Glencoe Literature.***

"The Drummer Boy of Shiloh" **(pages 310–319)**

In this lesson you will analyze and discuss the short story "The Drummer Boy of Shiloh," which is set just before a major battle of the U.S. Civil War. You will then create a slide show showing the connection of this story to its historical context—the Battle of Shiloh. Through your participation in the discussion and your work on the project, you will practice the following standards:

RL.8.2
RL.8.3 | ### Key Ideas and Details

- Determine the theme or central idea of the text and analyze its development.
- Analyze the relationship of the theme or central idea to characters, setting, and plot.
- Provide an objective summary of the text.
- Analyze how particular lines of dialogue or incidents in a story reveal aspects of a character.

RL.8.4 | ### Craft and Structure

- Analyze the impact of specific word choices on meaning and tone, including allusions to other texts.

Group Discussion

Discussing literature within a small group can help you grow as a reader and as a member of a learning community. Together, you and other group members can arrive at a better understanding of a selection, its ideas and craft, and its connection to other works and areas of study.

PLAN

RL.8.1
W.8.9, a
W.8.10
L.8.1
L.8.2, c | To prepare for discussion, build your content knowledge by examining the selection in greater detail. On your own, write your answers to the questions that follow, using text evidence. You may also write additional questions about the selection that you wish to discuss with your group. Your teacher may review your answers before the discussion, so be sure to use correct grammar, spelling, punctuation, and capitalization.

RL.8.2 **Plot** A story's **plot** is its sequence of events. When you **summarize** a plot, you explain the main events and the most critical details in your own words.

1. On the lines below, summarize the plot events in "The Drummer Boy of Shiloh."

   _____

   _____

   _____

   _____

   _____

   _____

   _____

   _____

   _____

RL.8.3 **Character** A **character** is an individual in a literary work. An author may reveal a character's personality through direct statements about the character. An author can also reveal a character's personality through the character's words and actions and what others think and say about the character.

2. Describe the personality of the drummer boy. Give examples of two direct statements the author makes to reveal parts of the boy's personality. What are some incidents and lines of dialogue that reveal aspects of the boy's personality? Explain how each example reveals the boy's personality.

   _____

   _____

   _____

   _____

   _____

   _____

   _____

   _____

RL.8.2 **Setting** The time and place in which the events of a literary work occur are its **setting.**

3. Describe the setting of the story, citing examples from the text. What **mood,** or feelings, do you think the author wants this setting to produce? Give some specific examples to support your answers.

_____

_____

_____

_____

_____

_____

_____

_____

_____

RL.8.2 **Theme** The **theme,** or central idea, is the message about life that the author wants readers to learn. An author may not always state the theme directly. Instead the author may express the theme through what characters do or say, the description of the setting, and the plot's events.

4. What do you think the theme of this story is? Give examples of ways in which the author develops the theme through plot, character, and setting. Explain how each example helps develop the theme.

_____

_____

_____

_____

_____

_____

_____

_____

_____

_____

RL.8.4 **Word Choice Word choice** is an author's use of specific, vivid words to convey a particular idea or feeling. Word choice can also express **tone**, which is the narrator's attitude toward the subject, theme, or characters. For example, the tone may be objective, argumentative, or respectful.

5. Choose five specific and vivid words or phrases from the story. List them in the left-hand column of the chart below. In the other two columns, write the meaning these words and phrases create and the tone they express.

Words or Phrases	Meaning Created	Tone Expressed

RL.8.4

Allusion An **allusion** is a reference to a well-known character, place, situation, or another work of literature or art. Like word choice, an allusion can help create meaning or establish tone.

6. The title of this story is an allusion to the name of a song from the Civil War era. In the song, the drummer boy dies. Find the other allusion in this story. Notice the author that Bradbury mentions in that allusion. There is a selection in your textbook by that author. Find and skim the selection to get an idea of what it is about and what feelings it might bring out.

Why do you think Bradbury includes these allusions? How do they affect meaning and tone in the story?

_____

_____

_____

_____

_____

_____

_____

_____

_____

ASSIGN

SL.8.1, a Meet with your literature group to plan your discussion. Each group member should become the expert on one or two of the questions on pages 18–21. Each expert will then guide the discussion on his or her question(s). List the group members and the question(s) that each will become the expert on in the chart below.

Group Member	Question(s) to Present

To become an expert on your question(s), spend some extra time thinking about your question(s) and consulting the text for relevant details. Building on your question(s), write down one or two discussion points or related questions for group members to consider as they explore text issues.

_____

_____

_____

_____

_____

_____

DISCUSS

SL.8.1, a–d
SL.8.4
L.8.1
L.8.3

Break into your assigned literature group to conduct your discussion. The expert on question 1 should begin by reading aloud the question and leading the discussion in response. Follow this process for each question until you have covered them all.

Remember that literature groups contain room for disagreement. Healthy debate can help all members push their understanding to a new level. Use your time wisely so that you are able to discuss all the questions sufficiently.

In your discussion, follow the guidelines below.

Discussion Guidelines

- Come to discussions prepared. Be sure you have read the material and are ready to probe and reflect on ideas and evidence.

- Set and follow rules for cooperative and collaborative discussions and decision-making, defining individual roles as needed.

- Track progress toward goals and deadlines.

- Express your ideas clearly and with sound reasoning. Support important points with relevant evidence and well-chosen details from the text.

- Speak with formal English grammar and usage. Use precise words to communicate your ideas.

- Pronounce clearly, speak at the proper volume, and make eye contact with audience members.

- Listen carefully so that you are able to pose questions that connect the ideas of several speakers and respond to others' questions with relevant evidence, observations, and ideas.

- Think about each speaker's ideas and claims. Is the reasoning sound? Is there enough evidence? Is there information that is not relevant?

- Acknowledge new information, and, when appropriate, qualify or justify your own views on the basis of the new evidence.

At the end of your discussion, be prepared to share the insights you have gained with your class. On the lines below, briefly summarize the most interesting ideas or insights you heard or experienced during the discussion.

_____

_____

_____

_____

The Drummer Boy of Shiloh

Ray Bradbury

21ˢᵗ Century Skills Project **Slide Show**

Now that you have analyzed and discussed "The Drummer Boy of Shiloh" in detail, you will have the opportunity to extend your thinking about it creatively by participating in a group project. Your assignment is to research and display images related to the theme of the story. If resources allow, you can use computer software to present your findings in a slide show.

PART 1. Gather Images Related to the Story's Theme

W.8.7
W.8.8

Conduct Research In a small group, come up with a statement of the theme of "The Drummer Boy of Shiloh" and discuss that theme. (Revisit your notes from your earlier discussion about the theme of the story.) Then conduct research to find images from the Battle of Shiloh related to the story's theme. Ask yourself which images best and fully represent the Battle of Shiloh. Because the battle is of such historical importance, you should find a wide range of images.

Use a variety of reliable print and online sources for your search. Search for photos, illustrations, political cartoons, and any other images you find relevant. As you do your research, look also for facts and quotations to support the theme. These will be part of the narration of your presentation. Here are some ideas for types of sources to consider.

- books about the Civil War
- historical archives
- university archives
- newspaper and magazine archives
- museum archives

Begin by gathering images and photocopying from books and magazines. If a computer is available, print images from online sources or download these images and store them on your computer. Use a chart like the one below to record each image and its source.

Image Name or Description	Source

Evaluate the Images After you have chosen a range of appropriate images, evaluate them according to how effectively they tell the story of the battle and illustrate the story's theme. Think about the following to fill out the chart.

- what the image shows
- what effect the creator of the image may have intended
- how the image relates to the story's theme

Image Name or Description	What It Shows	Creator's Possible Intent	Relation to Theme

21st Century Skills Project

21st Century Skills Project

Organize Your Images On your chart, highlight or circle the images your group decides to use. Then organize your images so you can make your point most clearly. For example, do you want to show images of officers first, then soldiers, then a drummer boy, then battle pictures, and finally images of the results of the Battle of Shiloh? On your chart, number the images in the order you would like them to appear in your presentation.

W.8.4 **Write the Text** Write a short introduction presenting your statement of the story's theme and the full message it conveys. Then decide which quotations from the story or historical facts fit best with each individual image. Finally, write a conclusion for your presentation. For the best results, you may want to go back and forth between organizing your images and writing your text. Make sure your writing maintains a formal style and an objective tone, and is appropriate to your purpose and audience.

Present Your Image Project If you are not going on to Part 2 of this 21st Century Skills project, your teacher may ask you to present your image show as the concluding activity of the project. You may also be evaluated on the presentation. Work with your group to compile your images and text into a suitable presentation display format. You might consider using a presentation board or book format. Be sure to cite your source for each image. Refer to pages R15–R17 in your textbook for citation guidelines. Once you have completed the format for your presentation, share it with your teacher.

PART 2 Create a Slide Show

SL 8.5
SL 8.6
After your group has finished Part 1 of this project, create a computer slide show with the images and text of your presentation. Label each image with its correct source information. Consider what multimedia elements you can use to clarify information, strengthen evidence, and add interest to your presentation. For example, you might create a voiceover of your written text to go along with your slides, using your opening and closing paragraphs as well as the relevant facts and quotations you gathered. You might also add music to establish the mood of your slide show. Answer the following questions to help guide you.

1. In what sequence will we present our slides to best express our message?

_____

_____

_____

_____

2. How long should we show each image? Should we show certain images for a longer time to achieve a dramatic effect?

_____

_____

_____

_____

3. What do we want the voiceover to add to the effect of our slide show? Should the voiceover be recorded or spoken live? Should it be by one person or by a number of people? Should the language be formal, or should it change depending on the content discussed?

_____

_____

_____

_____

4. What do we want to achieve with our music? What music should we use, and how should we play it in relation to our images? Should we include any other audio, such as sounds of battle?

_____

_____

_____

_____

5. What type of software will we use to present our slide show?

_____

_____

_____

_____

21st Century Skills Project

6. List the members of your group and the tasks each person will complete. Some tasks will need the help of more than one person.

Name	Tasks

SL.8.4 **Present Your Slide Show** If you do not create a voiceover for your slide show, decide with your group where and when you will incorporate spoken text. Remember that as you present, you should read each fact and quotation with the appropriate emotion and body language, making eye contact with your audience, speaking at an adequate volume, and pronouncing everything clearly.

Rehearse your presentation with your group. Practice presenting it to a small group of classmates, friends, or family members. Check to be sure that each member knows his or her role in the presentation and make sure that the presentation flows smoothly from one part and one member to the next. Make sure that you are presenting relevant information—both in your images and in your writing—in a focused manner that is easy for your audience to follow and understand.

Revise and strengthen any parts that are not working well or that seem weak, and adapt your speech according to the context. Then present your slide show to your class.

After you've completed the presentation of your slide show, answer the following questions.

1. What worked well in your slide show? What areas did not work as well as planned and could use improvement? Explain.

_____

_____

_____

_____

_____

21st Century Skills Project

2. How well does your slide show offer powerful quotations and facts that help explain how each image addresses the story's theme? Explain.

_____

_____

_____

_____

3. How might you change your approach to research, organization, and presentation if you were to do this project again? Why?

_____

_____

_____

_____

 SL 8.1 SL 8.2 **Observe, Analyze, and Evaluate** As you view your classmates' slide shows, take notes about content and effectiveness. Then use your notes to participate in a class discussion about the slide shows.

1. What main idea is presented in the slide show?

_____

_____

_____

2. Which images and text are most effective? Did all of the images reflect the story's theme, or were there some that were not relevant? Did the presenters provide enough and sufficient reasoning to explain how the images connect to the theme?

_____

_____

_____

_____

21st Century Skills Project

3. How does the overall choice and organization of images and text reflect the presenters' motive? How does it affect the quality of the slide show?

_____

_____

_____

_____

_____

4. What would you add or change in the slide show? Why?

_____

_____

_____

_____

_____

21st Century Skills Project

O Captain! My Captain!

Walt Whitman

Glencoe Literature, pages 640–645

RL.8.10 Before starting the lesson, read the following selection and complete the lesson activities in **Glencoe Literature.**

"O Captain! My Captain!" (pages 640–645)

In this lesson you will analyze and discuss the poem "O Captain! My Captain!" You will then perform a dramatic reading of this poem or other patriotic poems that are based on U.S. history. You may be asked to create a Web site that shows your performance along with media elements that support the reading. Through your participation in the discussion and your work on the project, you will practice the following standards:

RL.8.2 **Key Ideas and Details**
- Provide an objective summary of the text.

RL.8.4 **Craft and Structure**
- Determine the meaning of words and phrases as they are used in a text, including figurative meanings.
- Analyze the impact of specific word choices on meaning and tone.

Group Discussion

Discussing literature within a small group can help you grow as a reader and as a member of a learning community. Together, you and other group members can arrive at a better understanding of a selection, its ideas and craft, and its connection to other works and areas of study.

PLAN

RL.8.1
W.8.9, a
W.8.10
L.8.1
L.8.2, c
To prepare for discussion, build your content knowledge by examining the selection in greater detail. On your own, write your answers to the questions that follow, using text evidence. Make inferences about the text as you need to. You may also write additional questions about the selection that you wish to discuss with your group. Your teacher may review your answers before the discussion, so be sure to use correct grammar, spelling, punctuation, and capitalization.

RL.8.2 | **Summary** When you **summarize,** you explain the main ideas or events and the most important details of a text in your own words.

1. On the lines below, summarize what the speaker is saying in "O Captain! My Captain!" As you write your summary, consider the literal, or directly stated, meaning of the words in the poem. Remember, a summary does not include your opinions.

_____

_____

_____

_____

_____

_____

_____

_____

_____

Historical Context A writer may set a poem in a particular historical period. Knowing the historical context helps you to understand the poem.

2. Review Build Background for this poem in *Glencoe Literature,* page 640. Also, read Build Background and Meet Abraham Lincoln on page 504 in the lesson for The Gettysburg Address. Using what you have read and what you already know about the historical period, describe the historical context of the poem.

_____

_____

_____

_____

_____

_____

RL.8.4
L.8.5, a

Figurative Language Language that is not literally true but that expresses some truth beyond the literal level is called **figurative language**. A **metaphor** is a type of figurative language in which seemingly unlike things are compared without using the words *like* or *as*. An **extended metaphor** is one that an author uses throughout a literary work. It gives readers the chance to think more deeply about the comparison being made.

To identify the parts of the extended metaphor in "O Captain! My Captain!," note the images and ideas the poet repeats. Use what you know about the poem's historical context to understand the metaphor.

3. What evidence can you give to show that "The Captain" in the poem's extended metaphor is President Lincoln?

_____

_____

_____

_____

4. Use the chart below to show what the following words in the poem represent. Base your explanation on the poem and its historical context.

Words	What They Represent	Explanation
"our fearful trip"		
"the prize we won"		
"the ship is anchored safe and sound"		

Group Discussion

RL.8.4 **Word Choice** **Word choice** is a writer's use of specific, vivid words to express a certain meaning or feeling. Word choice can also express **tone**—the speaker's attitude toward the subject, theme, or characters. For example, the tone may be sympathetic, humorous, or objective.

5. Choose three words or phrases in the poem that you feel contribute to the poem's meaning and tone. For each word or phrase you've chosen, explain how the word choice contributes to the meaning and tone of the poem.

_____

_____

_____

_____

_____

_____

_____

_____

_____

_____

ASSIGN

SL.8.1, a Meet with your literature group to plan your discussion. Each group member should become the expert on one of the questions on pages 32–34. Each expert will then guide the discussion on his or her question. List the group members and the question that each will become an expert on in the chart below.

Group Member	Question to Present

To become an expert on your question, spend some extra time thinking about it and consulting the text for relevant details. Building on your question, write down one or two discussion points or related questions for group members to consider as they explore text issues.

_____

_____

_____

_____

_____

_____

DISCUSS

SL.8.1a–d
SL.8.4
L.8.1
L.8.3

Break into your assigned literature group to conduct your discussion. The expert for question 1 should begin by reading aloud the question and leading the discussion in response. Follow this process for each question until you have covered them all.

Remember that literature groups contain room for disagreement. Healthy debate can help all members push their understanding to a new level. Use your time wisely so that you are able to discuss all the questions sufficiently.

In your discussion, follow the guidelines below.

Discussion Guidelines

- Come to discussions prepared. Be sure you have read the material and are ready to probe and reflect on ideas and evidence.

- Set and follow rules for cooperative and collaborative discussions and decision-making, defining individual roles as needed.

- Track progress toward goals and deadlines.

- Express your ideas clearly and with sound reasoning. Support important points with relevant evidence and well-chosen details from the text.

- Speak with formal English grammar and usage. Use precise words to communicate your ideas.

- Pronounce clearly, speak at the proper volume, and make eye contact with audience members.

- Listen carefully so that you are able to pose questions that connect the ideas of several speakers and respond to others' questions with relevant evidence, observations, and ideas.

- Think about each speaker's ideas and claims. Is the reasoning sound? Is there enough evidence? Is there information that is not relevant?

- Acknowledge new information, and, when appropriate, qualify or justify your own views on the basis of the new evidence.

At the end of your discussion, be prepared to share the insights you have gained with your class. On the lines below, briefly summarize the most interesting ideas or insights you heard or experienced during the discussion.

_____

_____

_____

_____

_____

O Captain! My Captain!
Walt Whitman

21st Century Skills Project — Dramatic Presentation of a Poem

Now that you have analyzed and discussed "O Captain! My Captain!," you will extend your thinking about it creatively by participating in a group project. Your assignment is to read two other patriotic American poems and choose "O Captain! My Captain!" or one of the other two to present as a dramatic group reading. You may be asked to create a Web page that features your dramatic reading along with other media elements, such as pictures, videos, and sounds.

PART 1 Read Poems, Write Summaries, and Discuss

With a small group, read patriotic American poems. Then write summaries of each one.

RL.8.2 | **Read Patriotic Poems** Read the patriotic American poems "Barbara Frietchie" (page 100) and "Paul Revere's Ride" (page 338) in your textbook. You may choose to read the poems as a group or individually. After you read, write a brief summary of each poem. Then discuss the pros and cons of using that poem for your group's dramatic reading. Use the chart on the next page to takes notes as your group discusses.

Poem	Summary	Pros and Cons for Dramatic Reading
"O Captain! My Captain!"		Pros: Cons:
"Barbara Frietchie"		Pros: Cons:
"Paul Revere's Ride"		Pros: Cons:

SL.8.1, a **Choose a Poem to Present** After you finish discussing the pros and cons of presenting each poem, have your group decide on the poem you would like to use in your dramatic presentation. Discuss the following questions about the poem you choose:

1. Which group member will read each part of the poem?

_____

_____

_____

_____

21st Century Skills Project

2. What style of speaking would best fit the speaker or the characters of the poem?

_____

_____

_____

_____

3. What would be the best pacing, tone, and volume for each part of the poem?

_____

_____

_____

_____

4. What would be the most appropriate gestures and body language for specific lines of the poem?

_____

_____

_____

_____

5. What would be the best ways to express the tone of the poem?

_____

_____

_____

_____

Present Your Dramatic Readings If you are not completing Part 2 of this 21st Century Skills Project, your teacher may ask you to present your dramatic reading as the final activity of the project. You may also be evaluated on the presentation of your dramatic reading. Use your notes to guide you as you present.

21st Century Skills Project

PART 2 Record Dramatic Reading and Publish Online

After you have finished Part 1 of this project, meet as a group to video record your dramatic presentation. Discuss whether you will make any changes in which group member reads each part of the poem as well as the best style, pacing, tone, volume, and body language for your recorded presentation.

SL.8.4
SL.8.6
Record Dramatic Readings Video record a dramatic reading of the poem. Use your notes from pages 38–39 to help guide you. As you read your part of the poem, remember to use appropriate eye contact, adequate volume, and clear pronunciation. Adapt your speech to the context. For example, if the poem is written in a formal style, do not speak using an informal tone of voice. Remember to demonstrate command of formal English as you read.

SL.8.5
Build Your Web Page After you've recorded your dramatic readings, decide where you will publish your recording. You might publish on your school Web site. You can also search online for sites that allow you to post video, or create your own Web page for free. Consider adding media elements, such as music, sound effects, images, or video clips, to help enhance your presentation.

With your group, answer the questions below to help plan the online publishing of your dramatic presentation.

1. Where should we publish our presentation—on the school Web site or on another site? How will we post the video on the site? What software, if any, will we need?

   _____

   _____

   _____

   _____

2. What other audio, such as music or sound effects, could we add to strengthen our presentation?

   _____

   _____

   _____

   _____

21st Century Skills Project

3. What photographs, illustrations, and maps might help strengthen the presentation and add interest?

_____

_____

_____

_____

4. What additional video clips could we add to our presentation?

_____

_____

_____

_____

Publish and Present Using the answers to your questions as a guide, add any audio, graphics, or video that might enhance the presentation. Publish your dramatic reading of a patriotic poem on your chosen site. Then e-mail the URL to your teacher and classmates so they can read and view your work.

After you've published your dramatic reading of a patriotic poem, answer the following questions.

1. Did our presentation effectively communicate the message of the poem? Why or why not?

_____

_____

_____

_____

2. Which other media elements worked well with the presentation? Which did not work as well as planned? Why?

_____

_____

_____

_____

21st Century Skills Project

3. Which part of this project was most enjoyable? Which part was most challenging? Explain.

_____

_____

_____

_____

Evaluate View your classmates' work. Take notes about the content and effectiveness of their online dramatic readings of patriotic poems. Then use your notes to participate in a class discussion about the project.

1. How well does the dramatic reading express the poem's word choices, figurative language, message, and tone? Explain.

_____

_____

_____

_____

2. How well do other media elements highlight important words, phrases, and ideas in the poem? Does the presenters' use of media elements reflect a purpose or a motive? Explain.

_____

_____

_____

_____

3. How might the group improve the project?

_____

_____

_____

_____

Flowers for Algernon

Daniel Keyes

Glencoe Literature, pages 670–713

Group Discussion

RL.8.10 Before starting the lesson, read the following selection and complete the lesson activities in **Glencoe Literature.**

"Flowers for Algernon" (pages 670–713)

In this lesson you will analyze and discuss the short story "Flowers for Algernon." You will then write and publish a review of the story. Through your participation in the discussion and your work on the project, you will practice the following standards:

RL.8.2
RL.8.3 **Key Ideas and Details**
- Determine the theme or central idea of a text and analyze its development over the course of the text, including its relationship to characters, setting, and plot.
- Analyze how particular lines of dialogue or incidents in a story reveal aspects of a character.

RL.8.4
RL.8.6 **Craft and Structure**
- Analyze the impact of specific word choices on meaning and tone, including allusions to other texts.
- Analyze how the differences in the points of view of the characters and the audience or reader create such effects as suspense or humor.

RL.8.7
RL.8.9 **Integration of Knowledge and Ideas**
- Analyze the extent to which a filmed or live production of a story stays faithful to or departs from the text, evaluating the choices made by the director or actors.
- Analyze how a modern work of fiction draws on themes, patterns of events, or character types from religious works such as the Bible, including describing how the material is rendered new.

Group Discussion

Discussing literature within a small group can help you grow as a reader and as a member of a learning community. Together, you and other group members can arrive at a better understanding of a selection, its ideas and craft, and its connection to other works and areas of study.

PLAN

RL.8.1
W.8.9, a
W.8.10
L.8.1
L.8.2, c

To prepare for discussion, build your content knowledge by examining the selection in greater detail. On your own, write your answers to the questions that follow, using text evidence. Make inferences about the text as you need to. You may also write additional questions about the selection that you wish to discuss with your group. Your teacher may review your answers before the discussion, so be sure to use correct grammar, spelling, punctuation, and capitalization.

RL.8.3 **Character** A **character** is an individual in a literary work. An author may reveal a character's personality through direct statements about the character as well as through the character's words and actions and what others think and say about the character.

1. Describe the personality of Charlie. Give examples of two direct statements the narrator makes that reveal parts of Charlie's personality. What are some plot incidents and lines of dialogue that reveal aspects of Charlie's personality? Explain how each example helps reveal Charlie's personality.

_____

_____

_____

_____

_____

_____

_____

_____

_____

_____

_____

_____

_____

_____

RL.8.2 | **Theme** The **theme** of a literary work is its central idea about life. An author may sometimes express the theme directly. An author may also express the theme through what characters do or say, the plot's events, and the description of the **setting,** or the time and place in which the events of a literary work occur.

2. What message or theme do you think the author is trying to express in "Flowers for Algernon"? Give at least one example each of how the author develops the theme through character, plot, and setting. Explain how each example helps develop the theme.

Theme:_____

_____

_____

_____

Character:_____

_____

_____

_____

_____

_____

Plot:_____

_____

_____

_____

_____

_____

Setting:_____

_____

_____

_____

_____

RL.8.4 RL.8.9 **Allusion** An **allusion** is an indirect reference to another work of literature, music, or art, or to a well-known character, place, or situation.

3. "Flowers for Algernon" contains allusions to other texts. Each has an impact on the story's meaning and its **tone,** or the narrator's attitude toward the subject matter. For example, if Charlie mentions a children's book he is reading, the reader may understand that Charlie struggles with reading. The allusion may help create a sympathetic tone.

Use the chart below to record one of the story's allusions as well as its meaning and tone. Column 1 on the chart tells you the page number in your textbook where you should look for an allusion. In column 2, you will write the text mentioned in the allusion. You will record the meaning and the tone in the third column.

Page	Text Mentioned in Allusion	Impact on Meaning and Tone
699		**Meaning:** **Tone:**

Group Discussion

4. "Flowers for Algernon" has another allusion, this one to a story from the Bible (page 697 in your textbook). The allusion is to the story of Eve eating the apple from the Tree of Knowledge and God then sending Adam and Eve out of the Garden of Eden.

What does this allusion mean? How does the story "Flowers for Algernon" draw on themes, events, and characters from this biblical story? Describe how the story makes those elements new.

_____

_____

_____

_____

_____

_____

_____

_____

 RL.8.6 L.8.5, a **Irony** A contrast between the way things seem and the way they really are is called **irony.** In **dramatic irony,** the reader or audience has a different point of view, or perspective, from that of the story's characters, and the reader or audience has important information that the characters do not have.

5. Review the margin notes about dramatic irony in "Flowers for Algernon," Part 1. Then find three examples of dramatic irony in Part 2. Fill out the chart below to show what effect each incident of dramatic irony creates.

Examples of Dramatic Irony	What the Reader Knows that Charlie Doesn't Know	What Effect Is Created

ASSIGN

SL.8.1, a Meet with your literature group to plan your discussion. Each group member should become the expert on one of the questions on pages 44–47. Each expert will then guide the discussion on his or her question. List the group members and the question that each will become the expert on in the chart below.

Group Discussion

Group Member	Question to Present

To become an expert on your question, spend some extra time thinking about it and consulting the text for relevant details. Building on your question, write down one or two discussion points or related questions for group members to consider as they explore text issues.

_____

_____

_____

_____

_____

DISCUSS

Break into your assigned literature group to conduct your discussion. The expert on question 1 should begin by reading aloud the question and leading the discussion in response. Follow this process for each question until you have covered them all.

Remember that literature groups contain room for disagreement. Healthy debate can help all members push their understanding to a new level. Use your time wisely so that you are able to discuss all the questions sufficiently.

In your discussion, follow the guidelines below.

Discussion Guidelines

- Come to discussions prepared. Be sure you have read the material and are ready to probe and reflect on ideas and evidence.

- Set and follow rules for cooperative and collaborative discussions and decision-making, defining individual roles as needed.

- Track progress toward goals and deadlines.

- Express your ideas clearly and with sound reasoning. Support important points with relevant evidence and well-chosen details from the text.

- Speak with formal English grammar and usage. Use precise words to communicate your ideas.

- Pronounce clearly, speak at the proper volume, and make eye contact with audience members.

- Listen carefully so that you are able to pose questions that connect the ideas of several speakers and respond to others' questions with relevant evidence, observations, and ideas.

- Think about each speaker's ideas and claims. Is the reasoning sound? Is there enough evidence? Is there information that is not relevant?

- Acknowledge new information, and, when appropriate, qualify or justify your own views on the basis of the new evidence.

At the end of your discussion, be prepared to share the insights you have gained with your class. On the lines below, briefly summarize the most interesting ideas or insights you heard or experienced during the discussion.

_____

_____

_____

_____

_____

Flowers for Algernon

Daniel Keyes

21st Century Skills Project   Movie Review

Now that you have analyzed and discussed the story in detail, you will have the opportunity to extend your thinking about it creatively by participating in a group project. Your assignment is to view a film version of "Flowers for Algernon" and to write a review of the film with your group. In carrying out this project, you will follow the steps below:

- View and discuss the film.
- Write a review of the movie.
- If resources allow, create a blog to post your review and to accept comments and guest posts in response to your review.

PART 1 View the Film and Write a Review

View and Discuss As a class, view one of the film versions of "Flowers for Algernon," such as the movie *Charly* (1968) or the TV movie *Flowers for Algernon* (2000). Then, in your group, discuss your opinions about the movie.

RL.8.7
SL.8.1a, c

Write Your Review After discussing the movie, talk about the review you will write. Ask and discuss questions such as the following:

1. Would you recommend this movie to other people your age? Why or why not?

_____

_____

_____

_____

_____

_____

_____

2. What did you like about the movie? What didn't you like? Explain.

_____

_____

_____

_____

_____

_____

_____

_____

3. Do you think the movie did a good job of staying faithful to the story? Explain.

_____

_____

_____

_____

_____

_____

_____

4. Did the actors successfully portray the characters from the story? Provide examples to support your opinion. _____

_____

_____

_____

_____

_____

_____

_____

21st Century Skills Project

5. Did the director put the movie together in a way that you enjoyed—camera angles, lighting, movement of the actors, music, and so on? Did such choices by the director do a good job of reflecting the story? Explain.

_____

_____

_____

_____

_____

_____

_____

6. What is your overall conclusion about the effectiveness of the movie?

_____

_____

_____

_____

_____

_____

_____

Be sure to consider responses from everyone in your group. Pose questions that connect the ideas of several speakers and respond to others' questions and comments with relevant evidence, observations, and ideas. Then, with your group, use your answers and notes to write your review on a separate sheet of paper.

Present Your Movie Review If you are not going on to Part 2 of this 21st Century Skills Project, your teacher may ask you to present your review orally as the concluding activity of the project.

In your presentation, one group member can begin by summarizing the movie. Another can present the review. The remaining members can answer questions from the class. You may be evaluated on the presentation.

PART 2 Create a Movie Review Blog

After your group has finished Part 1 of this project, you may use your review to create a blog post.

A **blog,** short for "Web log," is an online journal created by one or more "bloggers." Bloggers write entries, or **posts,** on one or a variety of topics. A blog post may also include pictures, audio, and video.

A blog has a comments section where readers can share their opinions. In this way, the blog allows users to discuss topics and share opinions.

With your group, answer the questions below to help plan the creating of the post.

1. What kind of design do we want for our blog? How will we create this design?

_____

_____

_____

_____

2. Will we include images, music, other sounds, and video in our blog and post? How can we use this multimedia to clarify information, strengthen our claims, and add interest?

_____

_____

_____

3. What links should we include in our post?

_____

_____

_____

_____

21st Century Skills Project

4. What will we title our blog? What will we title our movie review post?

_____

_____

_____

5. What blogging service will we use that provides the most features we'd like to have but requires no fee to use?

_____

_____

_____

_____

Publish Your Blog Post After you've written your review on your blog, review it for content, creativity, multimedia features, group work, and communication of ideas. If you have time, make changes to strengthen any areas that seem weak. To publish your post, you click a "publish" button, and the post becomes public on the Internet. Do not publish until your teacher has read and approved your post. Then e-mail the URL for your blog to your teacher and class.

Invite other groups to post comments or guest posts on your blog in response to your review. Your group, in turn, may then want to respond to comments and guest posts.

After you've published your completed blog, answer the following questions with your group:

1. What worked well in your blog and why?

_____

_____

_____

_____

_____

_____

2. What would you change in the planning, creation, and presentation of this blog if you were to do this project again?

_____

_____

_____

_____

SL.8.1
SL.8.2 **Observe and Evaluate** As you read and view your classmates' blog posts, take notes about content and effectiveness. Then use your notes to participate in a class discussion about the blogs.

1. What main idea is presented in each blog post?

_____

_____

_____

_____

2. Which supporting information and images are most effective?

_____

_____

_____

_____

3. In what ways do music, other sounds, images, and video add to or take away from the effectiveness of each blog post?

_____

_____

_____

_____

21st Century Skills Project

4. What are the motives behind each blog post? Did each blog post accomplish what it set out to do? Explain.

_____

_____

_____

_____

5. What would you add to or change in each blog post? Why?

_____

_____

_____

_____

_____

_____

Group Discussion

The Diary of Anne Frank

Frances Goodrich and Albert Hackett

Glencoe Literature, pages 758–852

RL.8.10 Before starting the lesson, read the following selection and complete the lesson activities in **Glencoe Literature.**

The Diary of Anne Frank (pages 758–852)

In this lesson you will analyze and discuss the drama *The Diary of Anne Frank*. Then you will perform one scene from the play as Readers Theater. You may also videotape your performance and show it to your class. Through your participation in the discussion and your work on the project, you will practice the following standards:

RL.8.2
RL.8.3 **Key Ideas and Details**

- Determine a theme or central idea of a text and analyze its development over the course of the text, including its relationship to the characters, setting, and plot.

- Provide an objective summary of the text.

- Analyze how particular lines of dialogue or incidents in a drama propel the action, reveal aspects of a character, or provoke a decision.

RL.8.4 **Craft and Structure**

- Analyze the impact of specific word choices on meaning, including allusions to other texts.

RL.8.7 **Integration of Knowledge and Ideas**

- Analyze the extent to which a filmed or live production of a drama stays faithful to or departs from the script, evaluating the choices made by the director or actors.

Group Discussion

Discussing literature within a small group can help you grow as a reader and as a member of a learning community. Together, you and other group members can arrive at a better understanding of a selection, its ideas and craft, and its connection to other works and areas of study.

PLAN

RL.8.1
W.8.9, a
W.8.10
L.8.1
L.8.2, c

To prepare for discussion, build your content knowledge by examining the selection in greater detail. On your own, write your answers to the questions that follow, using text evidence. Make inferences about the text as you need to. You may also write additional questions about the selection that you wish to discuss with your group. Your teacher may review your answers before the discussion, so be sure to use correct grammar, spelling, punctuation, and capitalization.

RL.8.2

Plot The sequence of events in a story is called the **plot**. When you **summarize** the plot, you explain the main events and the most important details in your own words. You do not include your opinions.

1. On the lines below, summarize the plot of *The Diary of Anne Frank*. Remember to be objective and do not include your opinions in your summary.

_____

_____

_____

_____

_____

_____

RL.8.3

Dialogue The conversation between characters in a literary work is called **dialogue**. Much of the script of a drama is made up of dialogue.

2. Provide three examples of dialogue that propel the action of the plot or provoke decisions by characters. Explain why you chose each example.

_____

_____

_____

_____

_____

_____

Group Discussion

Setting The time and place in which the events of a literary work occur make up its **setting.**

3. Describe the setting of *The Diary of Anne Frank*. Support your response with vivid examples from the text.

_____

_____

_____

_____

_____

_____

_____

_____

RL.8.3 **Character** A **character** is an individual in a literary work. An author may reveal a character's personality through direct statements about the character as well as through the character's words and actions and what others think and say about the character.

4. Describe the character of Anne Frank. What are some plot incidents and lines of dialogue that reveal aspects of her personality? Explain.

_____

_____

_____

_____

_____

_____

_____

RL.8.2 **Theme** The **theme,** or central idea, is the message about life that the playwright wants audiences to learn. Theme may be expressed through character, setting, or plot.

5. What do you think the theme of this drama is? Provide at least one example each of ways in which the playwrights develop the theme through characters, setting, and plot. Explain how each example helps develop the theme.

Theme: _____

_____

_____

_____

Characters: _____

_____

_____

_____

_____

Setting: _____

_____

_____

_____

_____

Plot: _____

_____

_____

_____

_____

Stage Directions A script's **stage directions** describe the **set** (scenery and props), lighting, and sound effects. They also tell how characters should look and act. Stage directions often are italicized and enclosed in brackets.

6. Choose three examples of stage directions in *The Diary of Anne Frank*. Then fill out the chart below to show what each example reveals about the story.

Stage Direction	Page	What It Reveals About the Story

RL.8.4 **Allusion** An **allusion** is an indirect reference to another work of literature, music, or art, or to a well-known character, place, or situation.

7. This drama has an allusion to the story of the Maccabees from the Old Testament of the Bible (page 802 in *Glencoe Literature*). Summarize the allusion to the Maccabees. How does this allusion contribute to the meaning and tone of the drama?

_____

_____

_____

_____

_____

Group Discussion

ASSIGN

SL.8.1, a Meet with your literature group to plan your discussion. Each group member should become the expert on one or two of the questions from pages 58–61. Each expert will then guide the discussion on his or her question(s). List the group members and the question(s) that each will become an expert on in the chart below.

Group Member	Question(s) to Present

To become an expert on your question(s), spend some extra time thinking about the question(s) and consulting the text for relevant details. Building on your question(s), write down one or two discussion points or related questions for group members to consider as they explore text issues.

_____

_____

_____

_____

_____

DISCUSS

SL.8.1a–d
SL.8.4
L.8.1
L.8.3

Break into your assigned literature group to conduct your discussion. The expert on question 1 should begin by reading aloud the question and leading the discussion in response. Follow this process for each question until you have covered them all.

Remember that literature groups contain room for disagreement. Healthy debate can help all members push their understanding to a new level. Use your time wisely so that you are able to discuss all the questions sufficiently.

In your discussion, follow the guidelines below.

Discussion Guidelines

- Come to discussions prepared. Be sure you have read the material and are ready to probe and reflect on ideas and evidence.

- Set and follow rules for cooperative and collaborative discussions and decision-making, defining individual roles as needed.

- Track progress toward goals and deadlines.

- Express your ideas clearly and with sound reasoning. Support important points with relevant evidence and well-chosen details from the text.

- Speak with formal English grammar and usage. Use precise words to communicate your ideas.

- Pronounce clearly, speak at the proper volume, and make eye contact with audience members.

- Listen carefully so that you are able to pose questions that connect the ideas of several speakers and respond to others' questions with relevant evidence, observations, and ideas.

- Think about each speaker's ideas and claims. Is the reasoning sound? Is there enough evidence? Is there information that is not relevant?

- Acknowledge new information, and, when appropriate, qualify or justify your own views on the basis of the new evidence.

At the end of your discussion, be prepared to share the insights you have gained with your class. On the lines below, briefly summarize the most interesting ideas or insights you heard or experienced during the discussion.

_____

_____

_____

_____

The Diary of Anne Frank

Frances Goodrich and Albert Hackett

21st Century Skills Project Readers Theater

Now that you have analyzed and discussed *The Diary of Anne Frank* in detail, you will extend your thinking about the drama creatively by participating in a group project. Your assignment is to present a scene of the play as Readers Theater. You might also film the performance and present it to your class.

To complete this project, you will follow the steps below:

- Mark up a script for the scene you will perform.
- Discuss and rehearse the scene.
- Perform the scene as a Readers Theater.
- If resources allow, film your scene to show it to your class.

PART 1 Prepare Your Readers Theater

In **Readers Theater,** a group presents a performance by reading a script without using costumes or scenery. The readers use tone of voice, facial expressions, and meaningful gestures and stances to create an imaginary stage with interesting characters.

SL.8.1 **Choose a Scene** Each group in your class will perform a different scene of the play as a Readers Theater. Work with your group to identify the scenes you would most prefer to perform. Then meet as a class to discuss which group will perform which scene.

Plan Your Performance With your group, discuss your scene. Use the chart on the next page to write notes about the scene, the characters, and group member roles. Discuss these questions:

- What are the main events?
- Who are the characters featured in these events?
- Which group members will play which characters?
- Which group member will read the stage directions?
- Which group member will act as the director, advising performers about voice, facial expressions, and gestures?

Main Events	Characters in the Scene
Group Member Roles	

Read-Through As a group, read aloud your parts from the play. During the read-through, listen closely to each other's lines, paying attention to how each performer uses his or her voice. Provide constructive criticism to each reader.

SL.8.6 **Rehearse** Practice reading your part several times. As you read, try to "become" your character. Speak clearly and distinctly (unless the stage directions indicate otherwise), adding emphasis as needed. Adapt your speech and acting to the context as needed, trying different tones of voice and facial expressions to create emotion and suggest the location of your character. As you rehearse, consider your earlier discussions about the characters. Comment on each other's performances and mark your copy of the script as needed.

Present If you are not going on to Part 2 of this 21st Century Skills Project, your teacher may ask you to present your reading as the final activity of the project. You may be evaluated on both your individual and group work for the project.

During your reading, listen carefully to the other characters. Place yourself in your character's mind and imagine the events before you speak. Read lines at the right pace. After your performance, your teacher may ask you to turn in any notes or marked script passages you have.

21st Century Skills Project

PART 2 Film a Performance

SL.8.5 After you've finished Part 1 of this project, film your Readers Theater performance and present the video to your class. With your group, answer the questions below to plan the filming of your performance.

1. What equipment will we need? For example, are we going to use a computer and a digital video recorder? Is there other equipment we will need? Where will we find the equipment?

_____

_____

_____

_____

_____

_____

2. At what location will we film our scene? Why is that a good location?

_____

_____

_____

_____

_____

_____

3. How can we use our filmed performance to clarify information or add interest to the written play?

_____

_____

_____

_____

_____

_____

21st Century Skills Project

4. List the members of your group and the tasks each person will complete. Some tasks might need the help of more than one person.

Name   **Tasks**

_____   _____

_____   _____

_____   _____

_____   _____

Film and Edit Your Video Before your performance, be sure your video recorder is charged and ready to use. Record your performance. When you are finished, download and save the video.

SL.8.1 **Present Your Video** Present the video of your Readers Theater performance to your classmates and teacher on a computer or TV.

After you've presented your video, answer the following questions with your group.

1. What worked well when rehearsing, performing, filming, and presenting the Readers Theater?

_____

_____

_____

_____

_____

_____

2. What would you change if you did this project again? Why?

_____

_____

_____

_____

_____

_____

21st Century Skills Project

Observe and Evaluate Use the questions below to take notes as you view your classmates' performances. Then use your notes to participate in a class discussion about the project.

1. How well does the performance present the events? Do you think the actors and director were successful and made good choices in adapting the written play into a filmed performance? Why?

_____

_____

_____

_____

_____

2. Do the actors make any surprising choices, or choices you don't agree with? What are they? Why do you think they chose to present the scene this way?

_____

_____

_____

_____

_____

_____

3. What would you add or change to the filming of the performance? Why?

_____

_____

_____

_____

_____

_____

21st Century Skills Project

Reading Lessons: Informational Text

from Sojourner Truth: Ain't I a Woman?

Patricia C. and Fredrick McKissack

Glencoe Literature, pages 35–38

RI.8.10 Before starting the lesson, read the following selections and complete the lesson activities in *Glencoe Literature.*

"And Ain't I a Woman" (pages 30–34)

from *Sojourner Truth: Ain't I a Woman?* (pages 35–38)

In this lesson you will analyze and discuss the excerpt from *Sojourner Truth: Ain't I a Woman?,* by Patricia C. and Fredrick McKissack. You will then create a TV newscast about Sojourner Truth's speech, "And Ain't I a Woman?" Through your participation in the discussion and your work on the project, you will practice the following standards:

RI.8.2
RI.8.3

Key Ideas and Details

- Determine a central idea of a text and analyze its development over the course of the text, including its relationship to supporting ideas.
- Provide an objective summary of the text.
- Analyze how a text makes connections among and distinctions between ideas and events.

RI.8.4
RI.8.6

Craft and Structure

- Determine the meaning of words and phrases as they are used in a text, including connotative meanings.
- Determine an author's purpose in a text.
- Analyze how the author acknowledges and responds to conflicting evidence or viewpoints.

RI.8.8

Integration of Knowledge and Ideas

- Delineate and evaluate the argument and specific claims in a text, assessing whether the reasoning is sound and the evidence is relevant and sufficient.

Group Discussion

Discussing informational text within a small group can help you grow as a reader and as a member of a learning community. Together, you and other group members can arrive at a better understanding of a selection, its ideas and craft, and its connection to other works and areas of study.

PLAN

RI.8.1
W.8.9, b
W.8.10
L.8.1
L.8.2, c

To prepare for discussion, build your content knowledge by examining the selection in greater detail. On your own, write your answers to the questions that follow, using text evidence. Make inferences about the text as you need to. You may also write additional questions about the selection that you wish to discuss with your group. Your teacher may review your answers before the discussion, so be sure to use correct grammar, spelling, punctuation, and capitalization.

RI.8.2
RI.8.3

Main Idea The central idea of an informational text is called the **main idea.** Main ideas are supported by specific ideas and details. Authors use these supporting details to help make connections among ideas or events. They also use supporting details to show distinctions, or differences, between people, ideas, or events.

1. When you **summarize** a text, you explain the main ideas and supporting details in your own words. On the lines below, summarize the excerpt from *Sojourner Truth: Ain't I a Woman?* Do not include personal opinions in your summary.

_____

_____

_____

_____

_____

_____

2. How do the supporting ideas and details in the excerpt from *Sojourner Truth: Ain't I a Woman?* help the main idea develop over the course of the text?

_____

_____

_____

_____

_____

3. Do you think the authors make a clear connection between the struggle for women's rights and the struggle for the abolition of slavery? Why or why not? Give specific examples to support your opinion.

_____

_____

_____

_____

_____

_____

4. Do the authors show the distinctions between the opinions of Truth and those of the people who disagree with her? Explain your answers with examples from the text.

_____

_____

_____

_____

_____

RI.8.6 **Author's Purpose** An author's reason for writing a text is called the **author's purpose.** An author might write to entertain, to persuade, to describe, or to inform. Depending on what an author's purpose is in a text, he or she may need to acknowledge and respond to conflicting evidence or different viewpoints. For example, if the purpose is to persuade, an author may need to address opposing views to strengthen his or her own argument.

5. What was the McKissacks' purpose in writing about Truth's speech? How can you tell?

_____

_____

_____

_____

Group Discussion

6. Review Truth's speech on pages 32–33 of your textbook. What are two arguments that conflict with Truth's ideas? How does she acknowledge or explain those arguments? How does she respond to those arguments?

_____

_____

_____

_____

_____

_____

| RI.8.4 | **Connotation and Denotation** A word's **denotation** is its dictionary definition. Its **connotation** is made up of the thoughts and feelings associated with the word, often revealed by the context of a text.

7. Read the passages in the first column below, paying special attention to each word in italics. In the second column, write the denotation of that word. In the third column, describe the connotation of the word, based on its context in the selection.

Specific, Vivid Word Choice	Dictionary Definition	Connotation in Context
Some women came alone, but with their husband's or father's "*permission*." (pages 35–36)		
Soon the room was *buzzing*. (page 36)		
Some of the "*leading*" ladies were threatening to leave. (page 37)		
. . . these women together ought to be able to turn it back and get it *right-side up* again . . . (page 38)		

ASSIGN

SL.8.1, a Meet with your literature group to plan your discussion. Each group member should become the expert on one or two of the questions answered on pages 72–74. Each expert will then guide the discussion on his or her question(s). List the group members and the question(s) that each will become the expert on in the chart below.

Group Member	Question(s) to Present

To become an expert on your question(s), spend some extra time thinking about your question(s) and consulting the text for relevant details. Building on your question(s), write down one or two discussion points or related questions for group members to consider as they explore text issues.

_____

_____

_____

_____

_____

Group Discussion

DISCUSS

SL.8.1a–d
SL.8.4
L.8.1
L.8.3

Break into your assigned literature group to conduct your discussion. The expert for question 1 should begin by reading aloud the question and leading the discussion in response. Follow this process for each question until you have covered them all.

Remember that literature groups contain room for disagreement. Healthy debate can help all members push their understanding to a new level. Use your time wisely so that you are able to discuss all the questions sufficiently.

In your discussion, follow the guidelines below.

Discussion Guidelines

- Come to discussions prepared. Be sure you have researched the material and are ready to probe and reflect on ideas and evidence.

- Set and follow rules for collegial (cooperative) discussions and decision making.

- Track progress toward goals and deadlines.

- Express your ideas clearly and with sound reasoning. Support important points with relevant evidence and well-chosen details from the text.

- Speak with correct Standard English grammar and usage. Use precise words. Pronounce clearly, speak at the proper volume, and make eye contact with audience members.

- Listen carefully to classmates so you are able to pose questions that connect ideas of several speakers and respond to others' questions with relevant evidence, observations, and ideas.

- Think about each speaker's ideas. Is the reasoning sound? Is there enough evidence? Is there evidence that is not relevant?

- Acknowledge new information, and, when appropriate, qualify or justify your own views on the basis of the new evidence.

At the end of your discussion, be prepared to share the insights you have gained with your class. On the lines below, briefly summarize the most interesting ideas or insights you heard or experienced during the discussion.

_____

_____

_____

_____

Group Discussion

from Sojourner Truth: Ain't I a Woman?

Patricia C. and Fredrick McKissack

21st Century Skills Project   TV Newscast

Now that you have analyzed and discussed Patricia C. and Fredrick McKissack's excerpt from *Sojourner Truth: Ain't I a Woman?*, as well as Truth's speech "And Ain't I a Woman?," you will have the opportunity to extend your thinking about the selections by completing a group project. Your assignment is to write a TV newscast about Sojourner Truth delivering her speech. If resources allow, you can tape your newscast and publish it as a video podcast.

PART 1 Conduct Research and Write a Newscast

With a small group, you will research additional details about Sojourner Truth and her speech. You will use the information you gather to write a two- to four-minute TV news story telling viewers about the occasion for the speech, the content of the speech, and the audience's reaction to it.

W.8.7 **Write Research Questions** News writers make sure that the stories they write answer the basic questions *Who? What? When? Where? Why?* and *How?* As a group, write research questions to answer these six questions and to guide your research. Your first research question is given below. Think of at least five other research questions and write them on the lines that follow, leaving enough space to write answers to the questions.

1. Who was Sojourner Truth?

_____

_____

2. _____

_____

3. _____

_____

21st Century Skills Project

4. _____

   _____

5. _____

   _____

6. _____

   _____

Plan Your Research Have each group member focus his or her research on one or two of the research questions. To the left of each research question above, write the name(s) of the group member(s) who will find information to answer the question.

Gather Relevant Information Using only reliable print and online resources, such as the background information in your textbook and library or educational Web sites, conduct your research. Paraphrase your findings or write down direct quotations on separate sheets of paper or note cards. If you find additional information that you think will add to your news story, record that information as well. Remember to record the source information for each source you use. Refer to the Writing Handbook in *Glencoe Literature,* page R15, to see the types of information to record for each source.

W.8.7 W.8.8

Analyze TV Newscasts As a group or individually, watch several TV newscasts of various stories. As you watch, analyze the structure of each news story that is presented. Take notes to answer these questions:

- Who talks first about the news story—the news anchor in the studio or a reporter "on the scene"?

- Does the news story begin with the most recent development or with background information?

- What type of information is presented by the news anchor—general details and facts, his or her personal opinions? What images, if any, are on the screen while the anchor speaks?

- Where does the news story end—in the studio or on the scene?

- How does the story conclude?

21st Century Skills Project

SL.8.1 **Plan Your News Story** Discuss your research findings with your group. Review the key ideas presented about Sojourner Truth and her speech. Decide which pieces of information to include in your news story. Remember that you have only two or three minutes in which to tell the story, so keep only the most important details and discard the rest.

Next, use what you learned from your analysis of the TV newscasts to plan how you will tell the details of your story. In what order will you reveal details of the story? On the lines below, explain which details you will describe first, second, third, and so on.

_____

_____

_____

_____

_____

_____

_____

Assign tasks to each member in your group. Use the questions below to help you. Your group might add other tasks that aren't mentioned below. Some tasks will need more than one person. Use the lines on the next page to indicate who is responsible for each task.

- What newscast elements (news anchor, on-the-scene reporter, interviews, images) will you use to tell the news story?
- Who will take what roles in the newscast?
- Who will write each speaker's script for the newscast?
- Who will identify the costumes to be worn by speakers in the newscast?

21st Century Skills Project

Name	Tasks
_____	_____
_____	_____
_____	_____
_____	_____

Draft Your Story On separate sheets of paper, draft the parts of your news story following your plan. Then combine the parts of the script to create your complete story on a separate sheet of paper.

L.8.1
L.8.2, c
L.8.3

Revise and Edit Your Story After you have combined the parts of your story, ask the group members with speaking roles to read their lines aloud. Listen carefully and then revise any details, dialogue, or descriptions that are unclear or out of order. Check that the parts of your news story flow smoothly from one speaker to the next. Use transitional words and phrases to help viewers understand the sequence of events or a shift from one speaker or setting to another. Be sure you've used standard English grammar, and then edit the story for correct punctuation and spelling. Finally, write the final draft of your news story.

Present Your Newscast If you are not completing Part 2 of this 21st Century Skills Project, your teacher may ask you to present your newscast as the final activity of the project. You may be evaluated on both the written news story and the presentation.

In your presentation, be sure to speak clearly and precisely and at a pace similar to that in the newscasts you viewed earlier. Adjust your speaking style to fit individual roles. Change the tone or volume of your voice to communicate emotions of people being interviewed.

Once you have presented your newscast to the class, your teacher may ask you to turn in your written version.

PART 2 Film and Publish a Video Podcast

W.8.6

After your group has finished Part 1 of this project, you will videotape your newscast and publish it as a **video podcast**. A video podcast is online audio and video content that is made available to viewers through the Internet.

Prepare to Publish With your group, answer the questions that follow to plan how to make your video podcast.

1. What equipment will we need to gather?

_____

_____

_____

2. What video-editing or movie software will we use?

_____

_____

_____

3. Where will we film our newscast? Why is that place a good location?

_____

_____

4. Where will we publish the video podcast? Will we post it on our school or class Web site? Or will we find a Web site online that will let us create our own Web page for free?

_____

_____

W.8.6
SL.8.6
Film and Edit Your Video In your presentation, be sure to speak clearly and precisely and at a pace similar to that in newscasts you viewed earlier. Adjust your speaking style to fit individual roles. Change the tone or volume of your voice to communicate emotions of people being interviewed. Practice your presentation several times. Perform and record your newscast. When you are finished filming, edit your video file, and save it on your computer.

W.8.6
SL.8.5
Publish Your Video To publish your video, upload the file to the Web site you have chosen. Send the URL of your site to your teacher and classmates so they can watch your newscast.

After you've published your video, answer the following questions with your group.

1. What worked well when you were presenting, filming, and publishing the newscast?

_____

_____

_____

_____

2. What would you change if you did this project again? Why?

_____

_____

_____

_____

Observe and Evaluate Use the questions below to take notes as you view your classmates' newscasts. Then use your notes to participate in a class discussion about the project.

1. How well does the newscast present the details and emotions of the speech? Explain.

_____

_____

_____

2. What would you add or change in the video of the newscast? Why?

_____

_____

_____

_____

21st Century Skills Project

from The Great Fire

Jim Murphy

Glencoe Literature, pages 188–198

RI.8.10 Before starting the lesson, read the following selection and complete the lesson activities in **Glencoe Literature.**

from *The Great Fire* (pages 188–198)

In this lesson you will analyze and discuss the excerpt from *The Great Fire,* by Jim Murphy. You will then research and create a presentation about disaster safety measures. Through your participation in the discussion and your work on the project, you will practice the following standards:

RI.8.2 **Key Ideas and Details**

- Determine a central idea of a text and analyze its development over the course of the text, including its relationship to supporting ideas.

- Provide an objective summary of the text.

RI.8.4
RI.8.6 **Craft and Structure**

- Analyze the impact of specific word choices on meaning and tone.

- Determine an author's purpose in a text.

- Analyze how the author acknowledges and responds to conflicting evidence or viewpoints.

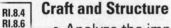

Group Discussion

Discussing informational text within a small group can help you grow as a reader and as a member of a learning community. Together, you and other group members can arrive at a better understanding of a selection, its ideas and craft, and its connection to other works and areas of study.

PLAN

RI.8.1
W.8.9, b
W.8.10
L.8.1
L.8.2, c To prepare for discussion, build your content knowledge by examining the selection in greater detail. On your own, write your answers to the questions that follow, using text evidence. Make inferences about the text as you need to. You may also write additional questions about the selection that you wish to discuss with your group. Your teacher may review your answers before the discussion, so be sure to use correct grammar, spelling, punctuation, and capitalization.

RI.8.2 | **Main Idea** The central idea of an informational text is called the **main idea.** Main ideas are supported by specific details.

1. When you **summarize,** you explain the main idea and its supporting details in your own words. On the lines below, summarize the excerpt from *The Great Fire*. Do not include personal opinions in your summary.

_____

_____

_____

_____

_____

_____

_____

_____

_____

_____

_____

_____

_____

_____

2. How do the supporting ideas and details in the excerpt from *The Great Fire* help the main idea develop over the course of the text?

_____

_____

_____

_____

_____

_____

_____

RI.8.6 **Author's Purpose** An author's reason for writing a text is called the **author's purpose.** An author might write to entertain, to persuade, to describe, or to inform. Many informational texts, such as *The Great Fire,* are written to inform. Part of the author's purpose in texts like these is to address conflicting evidence or viewpoints on a topic so that the reader gets all the information.

3. Review the first full paragraph on page 194. What are the two conflicting ideas that the paragraph expresses? Why is this conflict important to the account of the fire?

_____

_____

_____

_____

_____

_____

_____

_____

_____

_____

4. Does Murphy express his own opinions about the events he describes? Explain and provide examples. How does his writing style serve his purpose?

_____

_____

_____

_____

_____

_____

_____

Group Discussion

RI.8.4 | **Word Choice** A writer's use of specific, vivid words to express a certain meaning or feeling is called **word choice**. Word choice can also express **tone**—the writer's attitude toward the subject. For example, the tone may be sympathetic, humorous, or objective.

5. Choose three words or phrases in the selection that you find memorable. List the examples in the first column in the chart below. Then explain the meaning of each example in the second column and the tone of each example in the last column.

Word or Phrase, and Page	Meaning	Tone

ASSIGN

SL.8.1a Meet with your literature group to plan your discussion. Each group member should become the expert on one or two of the questions answered on pages 84–86. Each expert will then guide the discussion on his or her question(s). List the group members and the question(s) that each will become the expert on in the chart below.

Group Member	Question(s) to Present

To become an expert on your question(s), spend some extra time thinking about your question(s) and consulting the text for relevant details. Building on your question(s), write down one or two discussion points or related questions for group members to consider as they explore text issues.

_____

_____

_____

_____

_____

Group Discussion

DISCUSS

SL.8.1a–d
SL.8.4
L.8.1
L.8.3

Break into your assigned literature group to conduct your discussion. The expert for question 1 should begin by reading aloud the question and leading the discussion in response. Follow this process for each question until you have covered them all.

Remember that literature groups contain room for disagreement. Healthy debate can help all members push their understanding to a new level. Use your time wisely so that you are able to discuss all the questions sufficiently.

In your discussion, follow the guidelines below.

Discussion Guidelines

- Come to discussions prepared. Be sure you have researched the material and are ready to probe and reflect on ideas and evidence.

- Set and follow rules for collegial (cooperative) discussions and decision making.

- Track progress toward goals and deadlines.

- Express your ideas clearly and with sound reasoning. Support important points with relevant evidence and well-chosen details from the text.

- Speak with correct Standard English grammar and usage. Use precise words. Pronounce clearly, speak at the proper volume, and make eye contact with audience members.

- Listen carefully to classmates so you are able to pose questions that connect ideas of several speakers and respond to others' questions with relevant evidence, observations, and ideas.

- Think about each speaker's ideas. Is the reasoning sound? Is there enough evidence? Is there evidence that is not relevant?

- Acknowledge new information, and, when appropriate, qualify or justify your own views on the basis of the new evidence.

At the end of your discussion, be prepared to share the insights you have gained with your class. On the lines below, briefly summarize the most interesting ideas or insights you heard or experienced during the discussion.

_____

_____

_____

_____

_____

Group Discussion

from The Great Fire
Jim Murphy

21st Century Skills Project   Disaster Safety Presentation

Now that you have analyzed and discussed the excerpt from *The Great Fire* in detail, you will have the opportunity to extend your thinking about it creatively by participating in a group project. Your assignment is to research and write an outline about safety measures in a disaster. If resources allow, you will create a video podcast that communicates your findings.

PART 1   Conduct Research and Write an Outline

W.8.7
W.8.8

Conduct Research With a small group, discuss the excerpt from *The Great Fire*, with special emphasis on the safety measures taken to protect the people and property of Chicago from the fire. Then research other disasters to learn about safety measures the people and governments of those locations took. Choose one disaster as your group's focus, and use the information your group gathers to outline the safety measures for that disaster.

Conduct your research using multiple print and online sources. Be sure to use search terms effectively when you conduct research online. Assess the accuracy and reliability of each source. You might want to use some of the sources below to conduct your research.

- books about natural disasters in general
- books about a specific natural disaster, such as Hurricane Katrina
- weather archives
- historical archives
- university archives
- newspaper and magazine articles
- museum archives

21st Century Skills Project

Compile Information After you have studied a range of information about a particular disaster, compile information from your best sources in the chart below.

Disaster and Date	Article Title, Source, Date	Information About Prevention	Information About Safety	My Opinion

Outline Your Findings After you conduct research, get together with your group to organize your research findings. On a separate sheet of paper, outline the information you learned about safety measures in a specific disaster. Each major part of your outline should cover the following main ideas. Add details below the letters using numerals (1, 2, 3, etc.). Be sure to include specific examples and evidence, when appropriate. For help on creating an outline, see page R16 in your textbook.

I. Introduction

   A. What is the disaster? Where and when did it happen?

   B. What caused the disaster?

   C. What relevant safety measures were in place?

   D. What additional background information do people need in order to understand the disaster?

II. Problems

   A. What problems did the disaster cause?

   B. How effective were the existing safety measures?

   C. Were there additional safety measures that should have been in place?

   D. What safety measures were put in place after the disaster?

21st Century Skills Project

III. Solutions

  A. What lessons can be learned about disaster safety from this particular disaster?

  B. What can people do right now and in the future to help prevent a disaster like this from occurring again?

SL.8.4
SL.8.6

Rehearse and Present Your Outline If you are not completing Part 2 of this 21st Century Skills Project, your teacher may ask you to present your disaster safety outline as the final activity of the project. You may also be evaluated on your presentation.

Use your outline to orally present information about disaster safety. Meet with your group to choose which part of the outline each group member will focus on. Practice once before presenting to the class. Each group member should emphasize important points and back up ideas with details, examples, and evidence. At the end of the presentation, be sure to explain why the disaster and safety measures you researched can affect future disasters. Practice using appropriate eye contact, volume, and pronunciation, as well as formal English. Then present your outline to the class.

PART 2 Film and Publish a Video Podcast

After you've finished Part 1 of this project, film your presentation and publish it online as a podcast. A **podcast** is an audio or video file available on the Internet for people to listen to and/or watch. For this assignment, you will create a video podcast. Your class will publish all of its podcasts at the same online location, so people in your community can learn about disaster safety measures.

To begin planning your podcast, answer the questions that follow.

21st Century Skills Project

1. What equipment will we need? Will we need a computer and a digital video recorder? Is there other equipment we will need? Where will we find the equipment?

_____

_____

_____

2. What video-editing software will we use? Is the software already installed on the computer? If not, where will we find the software?

_____

_____

_____

3. Where will we film our disaster safety presentation? Why is it a good location?

_____

_____

_____

4. Where will we publish the video podcast? Will our class post its podcasts on our school or class Web site?

_____

_____

_____

_____

21st Century Skills Project

SL.8.4 | **Plan Text Features** To enhance your disaster safety podcast, incorporate text features into your video. Using video-editing software, you can create text to overlay on your video. You might create text for the following:

- the main ideas or sections of your presentation
- technical words that you want to define for viewers
- the names of each presenter

On the lines below, list words and concepts that you want to highlight using text features.

_____

_____

_____

_____

Film Your Presentation Before you film your disaster safety presentation, be sure your video recorder is charged and ready to use. Record your presentation. If someone makes a mistake, don't worry about it during filming. You can edit it out later. When you are finished filming, plug the digital video recorder into your computer and download the video into your video-editing software.

Edit Your Video Now begin the editing stage. First edit out any parts of your presentation that you don't want in your video. Then add your text over the appropriate parts of your video. Save the edited video on your computer.

Create Your Podcast Upload the file to the Web site your class is using. Send the URL of the site to friends and family, so they can learn about disaster safety.

After you've published your podcast, answer the following questions with your group.

1. What worked well when you were filming, editing, and publishing your podcast?

_____

_____

_____

_____

21st Century Skills Project

2. What would you change if you did this project again? Why?

_____

_____

_____

_____

SL.8.1 **View and Evaluate** Use the questions below to take notes as you view your classmates' podcasts. Then use your notes to participate in a class discussion about the project.

1. How well does each podcast present the topic of disaster safety? What suggestions might you offer to other teams?

_____

_____

_____

_____

2. How well do text features highlight main ideas, important concepts, and supporting details?

_____

_____

_____

_____

3. What would you add or change in each podcast? Why?

_____

_____

_____

_____

Saving Water

Marjorie Lamb

Glencoe Literature, pages 458–467

RI.8.10 | Before starting the lesson, read the following selection and complete the lesson activities in *Glencoe Literature.*

"Saving Water" (pages 458–467)

In this lesson you will analyze and discuss the persuasive essay "Saving Water." You will then stage a debate on the issue of water conservation. Through your participation in the discussion and your work on the project, you will practice the following standards:

RI.8.2 | **Key Ideas and Details**

- Determine a central idea of a text and analyze its development over the course of the text, including its relationship to supporting ideas.
- Provide an objective summary of the text.

RI.8.6 | **Craft and Structure**

- Determine an author's purpose in a text and analyze how the author acknowledges and responds to conflicting viewpoints.

RI.8.7
RI.8.8 | **Integration of Knowledge and Ideas**

- Evaluate the advantages and disadvantages of using different mediums to present a particular topic or idea.
- Delineate and evaluate the argument and specific claims in a text, assessing whether the reasoning is sound and the evidence is relevant and sufficient.
- Recognize when irrelevant evidence is introduced.

Group Discussion

Discussing informational text within a small group can help you grow as a reader and as a member of a learning community. Together, you and other group members can arrive at a better understanding of a selection, its ideas and craft, and its connection to other works and areas of study.

PLAN

RI.8.1
W.8.9, b
W.8.10
L.8.1
L.8.2, c

To prepare for discussion, build your content knowledge by examining the selection in greater detail. On your own, write your answers to the questions that follow, using text evidence. You may also write additional questions about the selection that you wish to discuss with your group. Your teacher may review your answers before the discussion, so be sure to use correct grammar, spelling, punctuation, and capitalization.

RI.8.2

Main Idea The central idea of an informational text is called the **main idea.** Main ideas are supported by specific ideas and details.

1. When you **summarize** a text, you explain the main ideas and supporting details in your own words. On the lines below, write a summary of "Saving Water." Do not include personal opinions in your summary.

_____

_____

_____

_____

_____

_____

_____

2. How do the supporting ideas and details in "Saving Water" help the main idea develop over the course of the text?

_____

_____

_____

_____

RI.8.6
RI.8.8

Author's Purpose and Argument An author's reason for writing a text is called the **author's purpose.** An author might write to entertain, to persuade, to describe, or to inform. In a persuasive text, a writer's purpose is to persuade readers to believe an **argument,** or opinion and reasoning on an issue. **Reasoning** is the writer's particular process of drawing conclusions from facts.

3. Write the sentence in which Lamb first states her argument. What are the claims she makes in her argument? What evidence does Lamb use to support her argument? Is her evidence sufficient and relevant? Explain.

_____

_____

_____

_____

_____

4. Read the following sentence from "Saving Water." Does it express a **fact** (a detail that can be proved) or an **opinion** (a personal belief)? Is it relevant to Lamb's argument? Explain your answers.

"Thanks to our treatment of water, chlorine has become an acquired taste in millions of households."

_____

_____

_____

_____

_____

_____

_____

5. Do you find Lamb's reasoning persuasive? Explain why or why not and support your answer with examples from the text.

_____

_____

_____

_____

_____

_____

Group Discussion

6. On page 463 of "Saving Water," Lamb suggests a conflicting viewpoint from her own. In what ways does Lamb respond to that viewpoint? Fill out the chart below to answer the question.

Sentence(s) Stating the Conflicting Viewpoint	Summary of Conflicting Viewpoint	Summary of Lamb's Response to Conflicting Viewpoint

Group Discussion

ASSIGN

SL.8.1, a | Meet with your literature group to plan your discussion. Each group member should become the expert on one or more of the questions answered on pages 96–98. Each expert will then guide the discussion on his or her question(s). List the group members and the question(s) that each will become the expert on in the chart below.

Group Member	Question(s) to Present

To become an expert on your question(s), spend some extra time thinking about your question(s) and consulting the text for relevant details. Building on your question(s), write down one or two discussion points or related questions for group members to consider as they explore text issues.

_____

_____

_____

_____

_____

_____

Group Discussion

DISCUSS

SL.8.1a–d
SL.8.4
L.8.1
L.8.3

Break into your assigned literature group to conduct your discussion. The expert for question 1 should begin by reading aloud the question and leading the discussion in response. Follow this process for each question until you have covered them all.

Remember that literature groups contain room for disagreement. Healthy debate can help all members push their understanding to a new level. Use your time wisely so that you are able to discuss all the questions sufficiently.

In your discussion, follow the guidelines below.

Discussion Guidelines

- Come to discussions prepared. Be sure you have researched the material and are ready to probe and reflect on ideas and evidence.

- Set and follow rules for collegial (cooperative) discussions and decision making.

- Track progress toward goals and deadlines.

- Express your ideas clearly and with sound reasoning. Support important points with relevant evidence and well-chosen details from the text.

- Speak with formal English grammar and usage. Use precise words. Pronounce clearly, speak at the proper volume, and make eye contact with audience members.

- Listen carefully to classmates so you are able to pose questions that connect ideas of several speakers and respond to others' questions with relevant evidence, observations, and ideas.

- Think about each speaker's ideas. Is the reasoning sound? Is there enough evidence? Is there evidence that is not relevant?

- Acknowledge new information, and, when appropriate, qualify or justify your own views on the basis of the new evidence.

At the end of your discussion, be prepared to share the insights you have gained with your class. On the lines below, briefly summarize the most interesting ideas or insights you heard or experienced during the discussion.

_____

_____

_____

_____

_____

_____

Saving Water

Marjorie Lamb

21st Century Skills Project   Debate

Now that you have analyzed and discussed the essay in detail, you will have the opportunity to extend your thinking about it creatively by staging a debate on the issue of saving water. In carrying out this project, you will follow the steps below:

- Do research to learn more about the issue of conserving, or saving, water.

- As you research, decide on a **proposition**—the statement of the point to be debated. You might use Lamb's argument as your proposition or you may choose a related or smaller-scale proposition, such as "Should we use water-saving appliances?"

- Search for evidence to support both the affirmative ("yes") and the negative ("no") version of your proposition.

- If resources allow, record your debate and post the audio online. Send the URL to another class, and allow them to offer comments and opinions.

PART 1   Conduct Research and Stage a Debate

With your group, conduct research into the issue of conserving water to prepare for a debate on this topic.

Conduct Research Use reliable print and online resources to find information related to conserving water. Answer the following questions to help guide your research.

1. What proposition will we debate?

_____

_____

_____

_____

_____

2. What kind of evidence will we need to find to support the proposition? What kind of evidence will we need to find to disagree with the proposition?

_____

_____

_____

_____

Organize Your Content After you've completed your research, divide your group into two smaller groups—one to argue in favor of the proposition and the other to argue against it.

Use the following outline to help you organize your points. Photocopy an extra outline for one of the groups. Then have each group fill out the outline in support of their argument.

Decide whether you want to open with your most persuasive point or whether you would rather end with your most persuasive point. Remember to support each point with evidence.

Topic: _____

I. _____

   A. _____

   B. _____

II. _____

   A. _____

   B. _____

III. _____

   A. _____

   B. _____

Plan the Format of Your Debate The **format** refers to the rules of the debate. For example, the speaker arguing the "yes" position usually speaks first and often gets to make the final statement as well. You can choose any format for your debate, as long as each group gets an equal chance to make its argument.

A debate usually has one speaker for each side, a moderator to introduce the debate and keep it running smoothly, a timekeeper, and a judge or judges to determine which side has made the best case. For this debate, the judges will be your classmates.

To plan your debate, think about these questions.

1. Who will be responsible for each task in the debate?

_____

_____

_____

2. In what order will the debaters speak? (In most debates, the affirmative, or position in support of the proposition, goes first.)

_____

_____

_____

3. How much time will each speaker get?

_____

_____

_____

4. Will each speaker get one opportunity for **rebuttal,** or contradiction, of the opponent's statements?

_____

_____

_____

21st Century Skills Project

SL.8.1a
SL.8.3

Prepare for the Debate As you get ready for the debate, prepare a checklist of questions to consider to help you respond to your opponent's argument. Use questions such as the following.

- What is my opponent's basic argument? Is the reasoning sound? Why or why not?
- What details and evidence does my opponent present to support the argument?
- Is any of the evidence irrelevant to the argument?
- Is my opponent responding to all of my evidence and arguments?

Present Your Debate If you are not going on to Part 2 of this 21st Century Skills Project, your teacher may ask you to present your debate as the concluding activity of the project. You may also be evaluated on the presentation.

In presenting your debate you should follow the format you planned and keep the debate running smoothly. Stick to the topic and time limits. Allow the class to ask questions of both sides before they vote for the winning side of the debate. Make an audio recording of your debate.

Once you have presented your debate, your teacher may ask you to turn in any notes you have assembled.

PART 2 Share Your Debate Online

SL.8.5   After you've finished Part 1 of this project, publish your recorded debate online in an interactive format.

Answer the following questions to help guide you.

1. Where should we post our debate—on our school's Web site or on another site that allows us to post for no charge?

_____

_____

_____

_____

_____

_____

2. How will we get the recording of the debate on the site? Will we need special software? If so, where can we get the software?

_____

_____

_____

_____

_____

3. How should we invite listeners' views and ideas—in a "Comments" link, as guest posts, or both ways?

_____

_____

_____

_____

_____

_____

4. Should we invite listeners to e-mail their views? Where can we set up a free e-mail account for this project?

_____

_____

_____

_____

_____

_____

_____

5. Should we respond to listeners' comments? In what format should we respond—through e-mail or on the site?

_____

_____

_____

_____

_____

_____

_____

6. List the members of your group and the tasks each person will complete. Some tasks will need the help of more than one person.

Name	Tasks
_____	_____
_____	_____
_____	_____
_____	_____
_____	_____
_____	_____

21st Century Skills Project

RI.8.7
W.8.6

Publish and Share Publish your debate on your chosen site. Send the URL of your site to another class either at your school or at another school. Allow the other class to post comments about the debate and to vote on the winners.

After you've completed this project, answer the following questions.

1. What are the benefits of presenting a debate in person? What are the benefits of presenting a debate online? Describe the advantages and disadvantages of using different mediums, such as Web sites and audio recordings, to present ideas.

_____

_____

_____

_____

_____

_____

2. Do the comments of the other class add to or detract from the debate? Explain.

_____

_____

_____

_____

_____

_____

3. What would you change in the planning, creation, and presentation of this project if you were to do it again? Why?

_____

_____

_____

_____

_____

21st Century Skills Project

Evaluate Listen to your classmates' recorded debates. Take notes about the content and effectiveness of each debate. Then use your notes to participate in a class discussion about the project. Think about questions such as the following.

1. How well has each group presented its debate? Explain.

_____

_____

_____

_____

_____

2. How effectively was the debate posted online? Explain.

_____

_____

_____

_____

_____

_____

3. Which delivery method—in person or online—best helped you understand the main points of the debate? Explain.

_____

_____

_____

_____

_____

21st Century Skills Project

I Have a Dream
Martin Luther King Jr.
Glencoe Literature, pages 573–581

RI.8.10 | Before starting the lesson, read the following selection and complete the lesson activities in **Glencoe Literature.**

"I Have a Dream" (pages 573–581)

In this lesson you will analyze and discuss the speech "I Have a Dream," which Martin Luther King Jr. gave in Washington D.C. at a crucial time in the Civil Rights Movement. You will then create a multimedia presentation with images, quotations, and text showing the connection of this speech to King's life and his work for civil rights. Through your participation in the discussion and your work on the project, you will practice the following standards:

RI.8.2
RI.8.3 | **Key Ideas and Details**

- Determine a central idea of a text and analyze its development over the course of the text, including its relationship to supporting ideas.

- Provide an objective summary of the text.

- Analyze how a text makes connections among and distinctions between ideas and events.

RI.8.4 | **Craft and Structure**

- Determine the meaning of words and phrases as they are used in a text, including figurative meanings.

- Analyze the impact of specific word choices on meaning and tone, including allusions to other texts.

RI.8.7
RI.8.8 | **Integration of Knowledge and Ideas**

- Evaluate the advantages and disadvantages of using different mediums to present a particular topic or idea.

- Delineate and evaluate the argument and specific claims in a text, assessing whether the reasoning is sound and the evidence is relevant and sufficient.

Group Discussion

Discussing informational text within a small group can help you grow as a reader and as a member of a learning community. Together, you and other group members can arrive at a better understanding of a selection, its ideas and craft, and its connection to other works and areas of study.

Group Discussion

PLAN

RI.8.1
W.8.9, b
W.8.10
L.8.1
L.8.2, c
To prepare for discussion, build your content knowledge by examining the selection in greater detail. On your own, write your answers to the questions that follow, using text evidence. Make inferences about the text as you need to. You may also write additional questions about the selection that you wish to discuss with your group. Your teacher may review your answers before the discussion, so be sure to use correct grammar, spelling, punctuation, and capitalization.

RI.8.2
RI.8.3
Main Idea The central idea of an informational text is called the **main idea.** Main ideas are supported by specific ideas and details. Authors use these supporting details to help make connections among ideas or events. They also use supporting details to show distinctions, or difference, between ideas or events.

1. When you **summarize** a text, you explain the main ideas and supporting details in your own words. On the lines below, summarize "I Have a Dream." Do not include personal opinions in your summary.

_____

_____

_____

_____

_____

_____

2. How do the supporting ideas and details in "I Have a Dream" help the main idea develop over the course of the text? Support your response with evidence from the text.

_____

_____

_____

_____

_____

Group Discussion

3. What distinction does King make between the promise of America and the realities of discrimination? Explain how this distinction is important to his main point. Support your answer with quotations from the speech.

_____

_____

_____

_____

_____

_____

_____

RI.8.8 **Argument** In a persuasive text, a writer's central idea is also his or her **argument**, or opinion and reasoning on an issue. **Reasoning** is the writer's particular process of using evidence and ideas to support his or her argument.

4. Write the sentence or sentences in which King first states his argument. What are the claims he makes in his full argument?

_____

_____

_____

_____

_____

_____

_____

_____

_____

5. Does King present enough evidence to persuade you that his argument is sound? Is the evidence related to his claims? Explain with examples from the speech.

_____

_____

_____

_____

_____

_____

RI.8.4 **Word Choice** Word choice is an author's use of specific, vivid words to convey a particular idea or feeling. Word choice can also express **tone**—the narrator's attitude toward the subject. For example, the tone may be objective, argumentative, or respectful.

6. Choose four specific and vivid words or phrases from the speech. List them in the left-hand column. In the other two columns, write the meaning these words or phrases create and the tone they express.

Specific, Vivid Word Choice	Meaning	Tone

RI.8.4 **Figurative Language** Language that is not literally true but that expresses some truth beyond the literal level is called **figurative language**. A **metaphor** is a type of figurative language that compares seemingly unlike things without using the words *like* or *as*.

King uses a number of metaphors in his speech. For example, on page 574, he refers to poverty as "a lonely island."

7. Use the chart below to show what the following figurative language in the speech represents. Explain your answer based on the ideas King expresses.

Figurative Language	What It Represents	Explanation
"a vast ocean" (page 574)		
"the dark and desolate valley" (page 575)		
"the quicksands" (page 575)		
"the solid rock" (page 575)		
"the high plain" (page 576)		
"a beautiful symphony" (page 579)		

Group Discussion

RI.8.4 **Allusion** An **allusion** is a reference to a well-known character, place, situation, or to another work of literature or art.

8. King presents an allusion to Abraham Lincoln's Gettysburg Address. Review that speech in *Glencoe Literature,* pages 506–507. Then find the allusion to Lincoln's speech in "I Have a Dream." Why do you think King makes this allusion? What effect does the allusion have on the speech's meaning and tone? Explain.

_____

_____

_____

_____

_____

_____

_____

_____

_____

_____

_____

_____

_____

ASSIGN

SL.8.1, a Meet with your literature group to plan your discussion. Each group member should become the expert on one or two of the questions answered on pages 110–114. Each expert will then guide the discussion on his or her question(s). List the group members and the question(s) that each will become the expert on in the chart below.

Group Member	Question(s) to Present

To become an expert on your question(s), spend some extra time thinking about your question(s) and consulting the text for relevant details. Building on your question(s), write down one or two discussion points or related questions for group members to consider as they explore text issues.

_____

_____

_____

_____

_____

Group Discussion

DISCUSS

SL.8.1a–d
SL.8.4
L.8.1
L.8.3

Break into your assigned literature group to conduct your discussion. The expert for question 1 should begin by reading aloud the question and leading the discussion in response. Follow this process for each question until you have covered them all.

Remember that literature groups contain room for disagreement. Healthy debate can help all members push their understanding to a new level. Use your time wisely so that you are able to discuss all the questions sufficiently.

In your discussion, follow the guidelines below.

Discussion Guidelines

- Come to discussions prepared. Be sure you have researched the material and are ready to probe and reflect on ideas and evidence.

- Set and follow rules for collegial (cooperative) discussions and decision making.

- Track progress toward goals and deadlines.

- Express your ideas clearly and with sound reasoning. Support important points with relevant evidence and well-chosen details from the text.

- Speak with correct Standard English grammar and usage. Use precise words. Pronounce clearly, speak at the proper volume, and make eye contact with audience members.

- Listen carefully to classmates so you are able to pose questions that connect ideas of several speakers and respond to others' questions with relevant evidence, observations, and ideas.

- Think about each speaker's ideas. Is the reasoning sound? Is there enough evidence? Is there evidence that is not relevant?

- Acknowledge new information, and, when appropriate, qualify or justify your own views on the basis of the new evidence.

At the end of your discussion, be prepared to share the insights you have gained with your class. On the lines below, briefly summarize the most interesting ideas or insights you heard or experienced during the discussion.

_____

_____

_____

_____

_____

I Have a Dream
Martin Luther King Jr.

21ˢᵗ Century Skills Project | Multimedia Presentation

Now that you have analyzed and discussed "I Have a Dream" in detail, you will have the opportunity to extend your thinking about it creatively by participating in a group project. Your assignment is to research and prepare for a multimedia presentation related to the central idea of the speech. If resources allow, you can use computer software to show your presentation to your class.

PART 1 Gather Images

W.8.7
W.8.8

Conduct Research In a small group, discuss the main, or central, idea of "I Have a Dream." Then conduct research to find images, facts, and quotations related to King's life to show the many ways in which that central idea influenced his life.

Use a variety of reliable print and online sources. Search for photos, illustrations, political cartoons, and any other images you find relevant. As you do your research, also look for facts and quotations to support the central idea. These will be part of your presentation. Here are some ideas for types of sources to consider.

- books about Martin Luther King Jr.
- photography archives
- historical archives
- university archives
- newspaper and magazine archives
- museum archives

Begin by gathering images and photocopying them from books and magazines, and (if a computer is available) by printing from online sources or downloading images and storing them in your computer. In the chart on the next page, record each image, its source, and its relation to the central idea.

Image Name or Description	Source	Relation to Central Idea

Organize Your Images In your chart, highlight or circle the images your group decides to use. Decide which fact or quotation you would like to present with each image. Then organize your images so that they flow together logically and help you make your point about King's central idea.

Write the Text Write a short introduction for your presentation explaining the speech's central idea and how it relates to King's life. Then write an appropriate fact or quotation beneath each image. Finally, write a conclusion for your presentation that sums up what you've presented.

Present Your Images If you are not going on to Part 2 of this 21st Century Skills Project, your teacher may ask you to present your images and text as the concluding activity of the project. You may also be evaluated on the presentation. Work with your group to compile the images and text into a suitable presentation format. You might consider using a presentation board or book format. Be sure to cite your source for each image, quotation, and historical fact. Refer to pages R15–R17 in *Glencoe Literature* for citation guidelines. Once you have assembled your images, share them with your teacher.

21st Century Skills Project

PART 2 Create a Multimedia Presentation

SL.8.5

After you've finished Part 1 of this project, use computer software to create a multimedia presentation with the images and text you assembled. If possible, add a **voiceover**, or audio narration, of your written text to go along with your images, using your opening and closing paragraphs as well as the relevant facts and quotations you gathered. You might also add music and other sound effects to set the mood of your presentation. Answer the following questions to help guide you.

1. What type of software will we use to create our multimedia presentation?

   _____

   _____

   _____

   _____

2. How long should we show each image? Should we show certain images for a longer time to achieve a dramatic effect?

   _____

   _____

   _____

   _____

3. What effect do we want to create through our voiceover? Should the voiceover be recorded or spoken live? Should it provided by one person or by a number of people? What emotions should the speaker express for each image?

   _____

   _____

   _____

   _____

   _____

   _____

4. What music should we use, and how should we play it in relation to our images?

_____

_____

_____

_____

5. How could we incorporate other audio, such as King speaking?

_____

_____

_____

_____

6. List the members of your group and the tasks each person will complete. Some tasks will need the help of more than one person.

Name	Tasks

RI.8.7
SL.8.4

Rehearse and Present Rehearse the presentation with your group. Practice in front of a small group of classmates, friends, or family members. Check that each member of your group knows his or her role in the presentation and make sure that the presentation is coherent, flowing smoothly from one part and one member to the next. If you do not record a voiceover for your presentation, read each fact and quotation aloud with the appropriate emotion and body language, making eye contact with your audience. Revise and strengthen any parts that are not working well or that seem weak. Then present to your class.

After you've presented, answer the following questions.

1. How well does your multimedia presentation address the central idea of the speech and how that idea was important to King's life? Do you include relevant evidence, valid reasoning, and well-chosen details? Explain.

_____

_____

_____

_____

_____

2. What are the advantages and disadvantages of using different mediums (images, text, voiceover, etc.) to address the central idea of the speech?

_____

_____

_____

_____

3. How might you change your approach to research, organization, and presentation if you were to do this project again? Why?

_____

_____

_____

_____

21st Century Skills Project

SL.8.1
SL.8.2

Observe and Evaluate As you view your classmates' multimedia presentations, take notes about content and effectiveness. Then use your notes to participate in a class discussion about the multimedia presentations.

1. What central idea does the multimedia presentation convey? What are the motives behind the presentation? Does the presentation achieve its purpose? Explain.

_____

_____

_____

_____

_____

2. Which images and text are most effective? Why?

_____

_____

_____

_____

3. How does the overall choice and organization of images and text affect the quality of the multimedia presentation?

_____

_____

_____

_____

4. What would you add or change in the multimedia presentation? Why?

_____

_____

_____

_____

TIME: Standing Tall

Michael Dolan

Glencoe Literature, pages 871–874

Group Discussion

RI.8.10 | Before starting the lesson, read the following selections and complete the lesson activities in **Glencoe Literature.**

"Standing Tall" (pages 871–874)

In this lesson you will analyze and discuss Michael Dolan's TIME article "Standing Tall." You will then create a multimedia presentation about skyscraper construction and safety. Through your participation in the discussion and your work on the project, you will practice the following standards:

RI.8.2 | **Key Ideas and Details**

- Determine a central idea of a text and analyze its development over the course of the text, including its relationship to supporting ideas.
- Provide an objective summary of the text.

RI.8.4
RI.8.5 | **Craft and Structure**

- Determine the meaning of words and phrases, including technical meanings.
- Analyze the impact of specific word choices on meaning and tone, including analogies.
- Analyze in detail the structure of a specific paragraph in a text, including the role of particular sentences in developing and refining a key concept.

RI.8.7
RI.8.9 | **Integration of Knowledge and Ideas**

- Evaluate the advantages and disadvantages of using different mediums to present a particular topic or idea.
- Analyze a case in which two or more texts provide conflicting information on the same topic and identify where the texts disagree.

Group Discussion

Discussing informational text within a small group can help you grow as a reader and as a member of a learning community. Together, you and other group members can arrive at a better understanding of a selection, its ideas and craft, and its connection to other works and areas of study.

PLAN

RI.8.1
W.8.9, b
W.8.10
L.8.1
L.8.2, c

To prepare for discussion, build your content knowledge by examining the selection in greater detail. On your own, write your answers to the questions that follow, using text evidence. Make inferences about the text as you need to. You may also write additional questions about the selection that you wish to discuss with your group. Your teacher may review your answers before the discussion, so be sure to use correct grammar, spelling, punctuation, and capitalization.

RI.8.2

Main Idea The central idea of an informational text is called the **main idea.** Main ideas are supported by specific ideas and details.

1. When you **summarize** a text, you explain the main idea and supporting details in your own words. On the lines below, summarize "Standing Tall." Do not include personal opinions in your summary.

_____

_____

_____

_____

_____

_____

_____

_____

_____

2. What evidence does the author include that supports the main idea? Does he change or refine this idea by the end of the article? Explain.

_____

_____

_____

_____

_____

_____

Group Discussion

RI.8.4 | **Technical Language** Words and phrases that are used by people in a certain job or area of study are called **technical language.** For example, when used in reference to sailing, the word *bow* refers to the front part of a boat.

3. Read the caption for the diagram on page 873. Based on the context, what do you think a *safety floor* is? Why would it be important?

_____

_____

_____

_____

4. Find three more technical words or terms in the article. Use the context to determine the meaning of each. Then explain how that term helps readers understand the main idea of the article. Use the chart below to compile this information.

Word or Term and Page	Meaning	How the Term Helps Readers Understand the Main Idea

RI.8.4 **Analogies** An **analogy** is a comparison between two things, based on one or more elements they share. In informational text, analogies are often used to explain something unfamiliar in terms of something known. Analogies can help contribute to the overall **tone** of a text, or the writer's attitude toward his or her subject.

5. Study the first full paragraph on page 874. What is the analogy at the beginning of the paragraph? What does that analogy help explain? How does this analogy help contribute to the overall tone of the article?

_____

_____

_____

_____

_____

_____

RI.8.5 **Text Structure** The patterns that authors use to organize information are called **text structures**. Some common structures include sequence, cause and effect, problem and solution, or order of importance. Paragraphs within a text also have structures. They begin with a topic sentence and include other sentences that develop the key concept in the paragraph.

6. Look again at the first full paragraph on page 874. Does the second sentence support the first, or does it add another point? Explain. What are the two main points of the paragraph?

_____

_____

_____

_____

_____

_____

_____

_____

ASSIGN

SL.8.1, a   Meet with your literature group to plan your discussion. Each group member should become the expert on one or two of the questions answered on pages 124–126. Each expert will then guide the discussion on his or her question(s). List the group members and the question(s) that each will become the expert on in the chart below.

Group Member	Question(s) to Present

To become an expert on your question(s), spend some extra time thinking about your question(s) and consulting the text for relevant details. Building on your question(s), write down one or two discussion points or related questions for group members to consider as they explore text issues.

_____

_____

_____

_____

_____

Group Discussion

DISCUSS

SL.8.1a–d
SL.8.4
L.8.1
L.8.3

Break into your assigned literature group to conduct your discussion. The expert for question 1 should begin by reading aloud the question and leading the discussion in response. Follow this process for each question until you have covered them all.

Remember that literature groups contain room for disagreement. Healthy debate can help all members push their understanding to a new level. Use your time wisely so that you are able to discuss all the questions sufficiently.

In your discussion, follow the guidelines below.

Discussion Guidelines

- Come to discussions prepared. Be sure you have researched the material and are ready to probe and reflect on ideas and evidence.
- Set and follow rules for collegial (cooperative) discussions and decision making.
- Track progress toward goals and deadlines.
- Express your ideas clearly and with sound reasoning. Support important points with relevant evidence and well-chosen details from the text.
- Speak with correct Standard English grammar and usage. Use precise words. Pronounce clearly, speak at the proper volume, and make eye contact with audience members.
- Listen carefully to classmates so you are able to pose questions that connect ideas of several speakers and respond to others' questions with relevant evidence, observations, and ideas.
- Think about each speaker's ideas. Is the reasoning sound? Is there enough evidence? Is there evidence that is not relevant?
- Acknowledge new information, and, when appropriate, qualify or justify your own views on the basis of the new evidence.

At the end of your discussion, be prepared to share the insights you have gained with your class. On the lines below, briefly summarize the most interesting ideas or insights you heard or experienced during the discussion.

_____

_____

_____

_____

_____

_____

TIME: Standing Tall

Michael Dolan

21st Century Skills Project Multimedia Presentation

Now that you have analyzed and discussed "Standing Tall" in detail, you will have the opportunity to extend your thinking about it creatively by participating in a group project. Your assignment is to research and prepare for a multimedia presentation related to the central idea of the article. If resources allow, you can use computer software to show your presentation to your class.

PART 1 Gather Images

RI.8.9
W.8.7
W.8.8

Conduct Research In a small group, discuss the main, or central, idea of "Standing Tall." Then conduct research to find images related to new skyscrapers and skyscraper safety since the attack on the World Trade Center in 2001.

Use a variety of reliable print and online sources. Search for photos, illustrations, diagrams, and any other images you find relevant. As you do your research, also look for facts and quotations to support the central idea. These will be part of your presentation. Sources to consider might include:

- recent books about skyscrapers, skyscraper construction, and safety
- recent newspaper and magazine articles

As you conduct your research, you may come across two or more texts that give conflicting information on skyscraper construction and safety. If this happens, identify where the texts disagree in interpreting facts or offering opinions and be sure to address these issues in your presentation. Remember that a **fact** is a statement that can be proven and an **opinion** is someone's personal viewpoint.

21st Century Skills Project

Begin by gathering images and photocopying them from books and magazines, and (if a computer is available) by printing from online sources or downloading images and storing them in your computer. Record each image, its source, and its relation to the central idea in the chart below.

Image Name or Description	Source	Relation to Central Idea

Organize Your Images In your chart, highlight or circle the images your group decides to use. Decide which fact or quotation you would like to present with each image. Then organize your images so that they flow together logically. For example, you might consider showing images of the tallest new skyscrapers first, then pictures and diagrams about new safety measures, and finally pictures and diagrams of skyscraper evacuations.

Write the Text Write a short introduction for your presentation explaining the article's central idea. Then write an appropriate fact or quotation beneath each image. Remember to address any conflicting information on skyscraper construction and safety. Finally, write a conclusion for your presentation that sums up what you've presented.

Present Your Images If you are not going on to Part 2 of this 21st Century Skills Project, your teacher may ask you to present your images and text as the concluding activity of the project. You may also be evaluated on the presentation. Work with your group to compile your images and text into a suitable presentation format. You might consider using a presentation board or book format. Be sure to cite your source for each image, quotation, and fact. Refer to pages R15–R17 in your textbook for citation guidelines. Once you have assembled your images, share them with your teacher.

PART 2 Create a Multimedia Presentation

SL 8.5 After you've finished Part 1 of this project, use computer software to create a multimedia presentation with the images and text you assembled. If possible, create a **voiceover,** or audio narration, of your written text to go along with your images, using your opening and closing paragraphs as well as the relevant facts and quotations you gathered. You might also add music and other sound effects to set the mood of your presentation. Answer the following questions to help guide you.

1. What type of software will we use to create our multimedia presentation?

   _____

   _____

   _____

   _____

2. How long should we show each image? Should we show certain images for a longer time to achieve a dramatic effect?

   _____

   _____

   _____

   _____

3. What effect do we want to create through our voiceover? Should the voiceover be recorded or spoken live? Should it be by one person or by a number of people? What emotions should the speaker express for each image?

   _____

   _____

   _____

   _____

21ˢᵗ Century Skills Project

4. What music should we use, and how should we play it in relation to our images?

_____

_____

_____

5. What other sound effects could we use?

_____

_____

_____

_____

6. List the members of your group and the tasks each person will complete. Some tasks will need the help of more than one person.

Name	Tasks

RI.8.7
SL.8.4

Rehearse and Present Rehearse your presentation with your group. Practice in front of a small group of classmates, friends, or family members. Check that each member of your group knows his or her role in the presentation and make sure that the presentation is coherent, flowing smoothly from one part and one member to the next. If you do not record a voiceover for your presentation, read each fact and quotation aloud with the appropriate emphasis, emotion, and body language, making eye contact with your audience. Revise and strengthen any parts that are not working well or that seem weak. Then present to your class.

After you've presented, answer the following questions.

1. How well does your multimedia presentation address the central idea of the article? Do you use relevant evidence, valid reasoning, and well-chosen details? Explain.

_____

_____

_____

_____

2. What are the advantages and disadvantages of using different mediums (images, text, voiceover, etc.) to address the central idea of the article?

_____

_____

_____

_____

3. How might you change your approach to research, organization, and presentation if you were to do this project again? Why?

_____

_____

_____

_____

21st Century Skills Project

SL.8.1
SL.8.2
Observe and Evaluate As you view your classmates' multimedia presentations, take notes about content and effectiveness. Then use your notes to participate in a class discussion about the presentations.

1. What main idea does the multimedia presentation convey? What are the motives behind the presentation? Does the presentation achieve its purpose? Explain.

_____

_____

_____

_____

2. Which images and text are most effective? Why?

_____

_____

_____

_____

3. How does the overall choice and organization of images and text affect the quality of the multimedia presentation?

_____

_____

_____

_____

4. What would you add to or change in the multimedia presentation? Why?

_____

_____

_____

_____

Writing Workshops

Writing Workshop

PERSUASIVE ESSAY

Glencoe Literature Connection: "The Trouble with Television," pages 468–474

Before starting the lesson, read the following selection and complete the lesson activities in ***Glencoe Literature.***

"The Trouble with Television," by Robert MacNeil (pages 468–474)

RI.8.10
W.8.1
W.8.9
W.8.9b
W.8.10

In this lesson, you will study the essay "The Trouble with Television" to discover how the author effectively uses persuasive argument writing methods and techniques listed below. You will then write your own persuasive essay using these methods and techniques. As you complete this workshop, you will practice the following standards:

W.8.1a, b **Develop Claims and Counterclaims**
- Introduce claims.
- Acknowledge and distinguish claims from alternate or opposing claims.
- Organize the reasons and evidence logically.
- Support claims with logical reasoning and relevant evidence, using accurate, credible sources and demonstrating an understanding of the topic or text.

W.8.1c **Use Transitions**
- Use words, phrases, and clauses to create cohesion and clarify the relationships among claims, counterclaims, reasons, and evidence.

W.8.1d **Establish and Maintain a Formal Style**
- Establish and maintain a formal style.
- Use the norms and conventions of persuasive writing and speaking.

W.8.1e **Provide a Conclusion**
- Provide a conclusion that follows from and supports the argument presented.

Analyze and Prewrite

Develop Claims and Counterclaims

Persuasion is writing that attempts to convince readers to think or act in a certain way. An **argument** is a type of persuasive writing in which logic and reason are used to try to influence a reader's thoughts or actions. In an argument, a statement of opinion about a problem or an issue is often called a **claim.** The support for a claim includes reasons and evidence. **Reasons** explain why someone should accept the claim. **Evidence** consists of examples, facts, and expert opinions. Evidence is relevant if it is related to your argument. In addition, the writer often anticipates and acknowledges **opposing claims,** or opinions from the other side of the issue. The writer then responds with **counterclaims,** or brief arguments that attempt to disprove opposing opinions about the problem or issue. Considering opposing claims and responding to them with counterclaims strengthens a writer's argument.

LEARN FROM THE MODEL

Skim "The Trouble with Television" in *Glencoe Literature,* as indicated below and on the next page, to see how MacNeil develops claims and counterclaims.

1. Use the chart to explore the claim, opposing claim, and counterclaim starting in the second paragraph on page 471 and continuing on page 472.

Claim:	
Opposing Claim:	
Counterclaim:	
Support for Claim and/or Counterclaim:	**Support for Claim and/or Counterclaim:**

2. What claim does MacNeil make about literacy on pages 472–473? What reasons or evidence does he use to support this claim?

_____

_____

_____

_____

_____

_____

W.8.1a, b   **APPLY WHAT YOU'VE LEARNED**

3. What topic will your persuasive essay be about? What claim(s) do you want to make about this topic?

_____

_____

_____

4. What reasons, evidence, and counterclaims will you use to support your claim? Use the outline form below and on the next page to create an organization that logically establishes clear relationships among claims, counterclaims, reasons, and evidence.

Essay Topic: _____

Claim: _____

I. _____

   A. _____

   B. _____

II. _____

   A. _____

   B. _____

III. _____

   A. _____

   B. _____

Argument

IV. _____

    A. _____

    B. _____

W.8.5
W.8.6
Peer or Adult Review Discuss your topic and outline with a classmate or an adult, or e-mail him or her your ideas. Ask for suggestions on how to improve your claims and counterclaims. Evaluate any suggestions and then revise what you've written or try a new approach.

Use Transitions

Good writers create **cohesive essays**. In a cohesive essay, the ideas in sentences and paragraphs are organized logically and linked clearly so the reader understands how each new paragraph relates to the argument. Writers use transitions to link the ideas in sentences and paragraphs. **Transitions** are words, phrases, and clauses that help clarify the relationships among claims, counterclaims, reasons, and evidence. Examples of transitional words and phrases that are useful in persuasive writing include *some people may say that, however, for instance,* and *for this reason.*

LEARN FROM THE MODEL

Reread passages from "The Trouble with Television" in *Glencoe Literature,* as indicated below and on the next page, to analyze how MacNeil uses transitions.

1. Reread the first paragraph on page 471. What transitional words or phrase does MacNeil use when he is establishing the relationship between what people are able to achieve and what television encourages? Is this transition effective? Why or why not? What other transitional word or phrase could MacNeil have used here to achieve the same purpose?

_____

_____

_____

_____

_____

_____

_____

Argument

2. Review the first two full paragraphs on page 472. Identify at least two transitions within this passage and explain how each one helps create a cohesive argument.

Transition	How It Helps Create a Cohesive Argument

W.8.1c **APPLY WHAT YOU'VE LEARNED**

3. Review your outline on pages 139–140. What words, phrases, or clauses would help make your transitions from point to point clear? Write down several possible transitions below.

_____

_____

_____

_____

4. Pick one claim from your outline and write a few sentences below using words, phrases, or clauses to clarify the relationship between this claim and its supporting evidence.

_____

_____

_____

_____

_____

Argument

W.8.5
W.8.6
Peer or Adult Review Discuss your sentences and transitions with a classmate or an adult, or e-mail them to your reviewer. Ask for suggestions on how to improve your transitions. Evaluate any suggestions you receive and then revise what you've written or try a new approach.

Establish and Maintain a Formal Style

In an argument, it is important for writers to maintain a relatively formal style so that readers think the argument is credible. In **formal writing,** you write from the third-person point of view and avoid using slang, contractions, or conversational language. Writers using a formal style should also use an objective **tone,** or attitude, so readers think the argument is reasonable. For example, if a writer presented an argument in favor of creating a secure bicycle parking area at his or her school and included a statement such as "School officials don't think enough students would ride their bikes, and that just doesn't make any sense at all, if you ask me," the reader would not be likely to take the writer seriously. The style is too casual and only presents the writer's personal opinion. The writer would sound more credible if he or she presented a strong reason for secure bicycle parking and used a more formal style. The following statement would be more effective: "Studies have shown that an increasing number of students would be willing to ride their bikes to school if there were a safe place to keep their bikes."

LEARN FROM THE MODEL

Reread passages from "The Trouble with Television" in *Glencoe Literature,* as indicated below and on the next page, to analyze how MacNeil establishes and maintains a formal style.

1. Reread the first two paragraphs of MacNeil's essay. How does he immediately establish his formal style? What words and phrases reflect this style? How does the information he includes contribute to the style?

_____

_____

_____

_____

_____

_____

Argument

2. Strong writers can introduce personal opinions and experiences into their persuasive writing while maintaining a formal style. MacNeil does this at various points in his essay. One example is shown in the chart below. Explain how MacNeil uses this personal reference while maintaining his formal tone. Then find another example in the text and explain its contribution to formal style.

Example of Personal Reference	How It Contributes to Formal Style
Page 473: problem symbolized "in my mind" by a certain type of television commercial	

W.8.1d **APPLY WHAT YOU'VE LEARNED**

3. Look at your outline on pages 139–140 and choose one paragraph to develop on the lines below. Focus on establishing and maintaining a formal style as you write.

_____

_____

_____

_____

_____

_____

_____

_____

_____

W.8.5
W.8.6
Peer or Adult Review Give a copy of your paragraph or e-mail the text to a classmate or an adult. Ask for suggestions on how to improve your formal writing style. Evaluate any suggestions you receive and then revise what you've written or try a new approach.

Provide a Conclusion

An effective conclusion in an argument should follow from and support the argument that the writer has presented. Strong conclusions often include a call to action or a comment that gives the reader something additional to consider.

LEARN FROM THE MODEL

Reread passages from "The Trouble with Television" in *Glencoe Literature,* as indicated below, and analyze how MacNeil constructs an effective conclusion.

1. Reread the last paragraph on page 473. How does MacNeil emphasize the importance of the problem as he sees it? How does he anticipate those who might not be readily willing to see things his way?

_____

_____

_____

_____

_____

_____

2. What call to action does MacNeil include in his conclusion? Do you think he has made an effective enough argument to justify the call to action? Why or why not?

_____

_____

_____

_____

_____

W.8.1e **APPLY WHAT YOU'VE LEARNED**

3. On the lines below, write down possible ideas for the conclusion of your essay. How will the conclusion follow from and support the rest of your essay? What call to action or additional thought will you include?

_____

_____

_____

_____

_____

_____

_____

_____

W.8.5
W.8.6 **Peer or Adult Review** Discuss your ideas for an effective conclusion with a classmate or an adult in person or through e-mail. Ask for suggestions on how to improve your conclusion. Evaluate any suggestions you receive and then revise what you've written or try a new approach.

Draft

W.8.10 Before you begin drafting, review your prewriting notes on pages 138–145. Then use a computer to write your first draft, following the instructions below.

W.8.1a, d **Write the Introduction**

Begin by writing the introductory paragraph or paragraphs of your persuasive essay. Your introduction should include

- your claim, or statement of your position on the issue, and your basic reason for making that claim
- a statement of what you want your reader to do in response
- a brief explanation of your main points and supporting evidence (or at least a reference to this context if you can assume your reader knows about it)
- an explanation of why your topic matters

Remember to establish a formal style in your introduction.

Argument

W.8.1, a–d
W.8.4

Write the Body

Use your outline to guide you as you write the body of your persuasive essay. Remember to support your claims with logical reasoning and relevant evidence. You should use accurate, credible sources for this support and demonstrate an understanding of your topic. You will also need to distinguish your claims from alternate or opposing claims. To strengthen your argument, be sure that you include counterclaims, or brief arguments that attempt to disprove opposing opinions. Create cohesion by using transitional words, phrases, or clauses to link the different claims and support.

You might wish to present claims, opposing claims, and counterclaims by using sentence frames like the following:

- Opponents to this issue say that _____, but the evidence shows that _____.

- Many people will probably disagree with my assertion that _____, because _____, but _____.

Be sure to develop claims and counterclaims accurately by supplying logical reasons and relevant evidence. Point out the strengths and limitations of your claims and counterclaims based on what your audience knows about the issue and concerns that they may have. Read the annotated model below to get an idea of how to present claims, opposing claims, counterclaims, and evidence.

Claim: Part of the faculty parking lot should be set aside for a secure student bicycle parking area.

Opposing View: Opponents of the student bicycle parking area state that this area would result in several lost parking spots for teachers, while not enough students would ride their bikes to justify that loss.

Counterclaim and Evidence: While it is true that many students do not ride their bikes to school now, several polls of students suggest that many do not ride now because of the lack of a place to park their bikes. In addition, the same poll reveals that many of these students are eager to ride to school.

Anticipation of Audience Concern: While some faculty parking spots would be lost, creating the secure parking area would encourage students to ride their bikes to school. The students would also be able to ride to school safely, given the number of bike paths around the neighborhood that lead directly to the school grounds.

Notice that the writer anticipates possible concerns from the audience about the student bicycle parking area by acknowledging the validity of the opposing claim ("While it is true that students do not ride their bikes to school now"). The writer then presents a solid counterclaim that is supported by evidence. The writer proceeds to anticipate further audience concerns about the safety of students riding their bikes to school by mentioning the number of bike paths that lead directly to the school.

As you write, make sure the structure of your essay establishes clear relationships among the claims, counterclaims, reasons, and evidence. Maintain the formal style that you established in the introduction.

W.8.1e | Write the Conclusion

Finally, write the conclusion of your essay. Make sure it follows from and supports your argument. Your conclusion could be a single paragraph, or it could be several paragraphs, depending on what you want to do in it. Following are some things a well-written conclusion can do:

- restate your main claim forcefully or with an added twist
- summarize your strongest claims
- present a final summary of all your ideas
- connect persuasively with your audience
- suggest next steps (for example, a call to action), questions, or areas of exploration

W.8.4 | Revise

To revise your essay, you will focus on the content, or message, of your writing and apply one or more of these four revision strategies:

- **Add** details and information to make the message clearer.
- **Remove** distracting or unnecessary words or ideas.
- **Substitute** more precise or stronger words for bland or overused language.
- **Rearrange** phrases and sentences to be sure the message is logically presented.

The questions that follow on the next page will show you how to use these revision strategies. They will help you consider whether the development, organization, and style of your essay are appropriate to your task, purpose, and audience.

Argument

W.8.4 | Focus and Coherence

Ask yourself the following questions. Then evaluate your essay and check each box when you can answer "yes" to the question.

☐ Does my essay have a clear focus?

☐ Is my writing coherent?

☐ Do all the parts work together so that I achieve my purpose?

W.8.1a, e | Organization

Ask yourself the following questions. Then evaluate your essay and check each box when you can answer "yes" to the question.

☐ Does the beginning introduce my argument and explain why it is important?

☐ Does the body follow an organization that establishes clear relationships among claims, counterclaims, reasons, and evidence?

☐ Does the conclusion follow from and support my argument?

W.8.1a, b / W.8.4 | Development of Ideas

Ask yourself the following questions. Then evaluate your essay and check each box when you can answer "yes" to the question.

☐ Do I introduce claims and distinguish them from alternate or opposing claims?

☐ Do I develop my claims and counterclaims fairly, supplying evidence for each?

☐ Do I present the strengths and limitations of my claims and counterclaims in a way that anticipates my audience's knowledge level and concerns?

Voice—Word Choice

W.8.1d / W.8.4 / L.8.3 |

Ask yourself the following questions. Then evaluate your essay and check each box when you can answer "yes" to the question.

☐ Do I use persuasive language?

☐ Do I establish and maintain a formal style?

☐ Do I use knowledge of language and its conventions when writing?

W.8.1c
W.8.4

Voice—Sentence Fluency

Ask yourself the following questions. Then evaluate your essay and check each box when you can answer "yes" to the question.

☐ Does my writing flow smoothly?

☐ Does my essay include transitional words, phrases, and clauses to create cohesion?

☐ Do I use words, phrases, and clauses to clarify the relationships among claims, counterclaims, reasons, and evidence?

☐ Do I emphasize important points?

W.8.5
W.8.6

Peer or Adult Review Share your essay and the checklists with a classmate or an adult. Have your reviewer use the checklists to evaluate your essay and offer suggestions for improvement. Discuss the suggestions in person or e-mail specific questions or responses to their comments. Next, revise your essay, as needed, possibly trying a new approach to cover areas of concern.

Edit and Proofread

L.8.1a
L.8.3

Correct Errors in Grammar

Editing involves correcting errors in grammar, usage, mechanics, and spelling. As you edit, make sure your work conforms to the guidelines in a style manual that is appropriate for this type of writing. Check with your teacher to see which style guide you should use for reference.

Begin the editing stage by taking a careful look at your sentences. Make sure that each sentence expresses a complete thought in a way that is grammatically correct. Use the checklist below to edit your sentences.

SENTENCE-EDITING CHECKLIST

☐ Have I avoided sentence fragments?

☐ Have I avoided run-on sentences?

☐ Do verbs agree with their subjects?

☐ Are pronouns used correctly?

☐ Are verbs used correctly?

☐ Have I avoided misplaced and dangling modifiers?

☐ Have I used phrases and clauses correctly?

☐ Have I used verbals correctly?

Argument

L.8.2c **Correct Errors in Mechanics and Spelling**

Next, check for and correct any errors in mechanics (punctuation and capitalization) and spelling. Use the checklist below to edit your persuasive essay. You should also use a dictionary to check and confirm spellings.

PROOFREADING CHECKLIST

☐ Are commas and other punctuation marks used as needed?

☐ Are all words spelled correctly?

☐ Are capital letters used as needed?

W.8.5
W.8.6
Peer or Adult Review Share your essay and the editing-and-proofreading checklists with a classmate or an adult. Have your reviewer use the checklists to evaluate your essay and offer suggestions for improvement. Discuss the suggestions in person or e-mail specific questions or responses to their comments. Next, write the final draft of your essay.

Present/Publish

W.8.6 After you have written and polished your persuasive essay, you will want to publish and present it so classmates, friends, and family can respond to it. You may wish to consider some of these publishing and presenting options:

- Present your essay orally to your class.
- Use your essay as a springboard for a class debate.
- Publish a multimedia version of your essay online with accompanying links and images.

Consider using technology, including the Internet, to publish your essay. Take advantage of the flexibility of technology, which allows you to type in text, move it around, make changes, and create a clear, logical display. You may wish to consult some of the projects in the Reading section of this book for additional publishing ideas that include technology.

Grammar Practice

L.8.1, a ### Verbals

Verbals are words that are formed from verbs but function as other parts of speech. There are three kinds of verbals: participles, gerunds, and infinitives.

Participles

A participle is a word formed from a verb that may also be used as an adjective. There are present participles, which end in *-ing,* and past participles, which end in various ways, such as *-ed, -en,* or *-t.* A participle may be part of a participial phrase that modifies a noun or pronoun in the sentence, or it may stand alone as an adjective.

Examples: I saw my brother <u>watching</u> TV. (phrase modifies *brother*)
His <u>chosen</u> show seemed silly to me. (modifies *show*)

To identify a participle, check whether the word that looks like a verb is being used as a verb or as an adjective.

EXERCISE A: IDENTIFYING PARTICIPLES

For each sentence, decide whether the underlined word is being used as a verb or as an adjective. Write **V** (for *verb*) or **A** (for *adjective*) on the line.

_____ **1.** <u>Sitting</u> on the sofa, I once watched hours of TV every night.

_____ **2.** Last night, I was <u>reading</u> "The Trouble with Television" instead.

_____ **3.** I realized that the essay was more <u>interesting</u> than I had expected.

_____ **4.** I hadn't realized that the <u>written</u> word could influence me so much.

_____ **5.** The essay was <u>written</u> by Robert MacNeil.

Gerunds

A gerund is a verb form with an *-ing* ending that is used as a noun. A gerund may be part of a gerund phrase. It may also, like a participle, stand alone as a subject or an object.

Examples: I enjoy <u>watching</u> some TV. (direct object of the verb)
<u>Reading</u> can be more interesting. (subject of the sentence)

To identify a gerund, check to see whether the word that ends in *-ing* and looks like a verb is being used as a verb, as an adjective, or as a noun.

EXERCISE B: IDENTIFYING GERUNDS

For each sentence, decide whether the underlined word is being used as a verb or as a gerund. Write **V** (for *verb*) or **G** (for *gerund*) on the line.

_____ **6.** <u>Concentrating</u> on TV prevents us from learning other things.

_____ **7.** I was <u>studying</u> the essay while the TV was on.

_____ **8.** The noise from the TV was <u>annoying</u> me.

_____ **9.** There is no substitute for <u>learning</u>!

_____ **10.** I read that <u>following</u> written instructions is hard for many adults.

Infinitives

An infinitive is a verb form, usually beginning with the word *to* followed by the verb, such as *to see* or *to run*. It is most often used as a noun but can be used as an adjective or adverb. When the word *to* is used to form an infinitive, *to* is not a preposition; it is just part of the infinitive.

Examples: I tried <u>to concentrate</u>. (noun, direct object of *tried*)

I have the desire <u>to learn</u>. (adjective modifying *desire*)

After a few hours, I was ready <u>to stop</u>. (adverb modifying *ready*)

EXERCISE C: IDENTIFYING INFINITIVES

For each sentence, decide whether *to* in the underlined phrase is being used as a preposition or as part of an infinitive. Write **P** (for *preposition*) or **I** (for *infinitive*) on the line.

_____ **11.** I started looking forward <u>to bedtime</u>.

_____ **12.** I wanted <u>to remember</u> what I had read.

_____ **13.** Would I remember the essay when I went <u>to school</u>?

_____ **14.** <u>To ignore</u> television is hard, but it can have great benefits.

_____ **15.** I went <u>to sleep</u> still wondering about that question.

Check Your Writing Read through your persuasive essay to make sure that you have included verbals—participles, gerunds, and infinitives—where they could be appropriately used. The major goal of writing is to communicate clearly and effectively, and the use of verbals can help you meet that goal.

Argument

Writing Workshop

RESEARCH REPORT

Glencoe Literature Connection: Franklin D. Roosevelt, page 734–735

Before starting the lesson, read the following student model in ***Glencoe Literature.***

"Franklin D. Roosevelt" **(pages 734–735)**

W.8.2
W.8.9,b
W.8.10

In this lesson, you will study the student model about Franklin D. Roosevelt to see how the writer effectively uses the informative/explanatory writing and research methods and techniques listed below. You will then write your own research report using these methods and techniques. As you complete this workshop, you will practice the following standards:

W.8.7
W.8.8

Conduct Research

- Conduct research to answer a question (including a self-generated question), drawing on several sources, and generating additional related, focused questions that allow for multiple avenues of investigation.
- Gather information from multiple print and digital sources, using search terms effectively.
- Assess the credibility and accuracy of each source.
- Quote or paraphrase the data and conclusions of others while avoiding plagiarism.
- Follow a standard format for citation.

W.8.2a, b

Develop a Topic

- Introduce a topic clearly, previewing what is to follow.
- Develop the topic with relevant, well-chosen facts, definitions, concrete details, quotations, or other information and examples.
- Organize ideas, concepts, and information into broader categories.
- Include formatting, graphics, and multimedia when useful to aiding comprehension.

W.8.2c, d

Use Transitions and Precise Language

- Use appropriate and varied transitions to create cohesion and clarify the relationships among ideas and concepts.
- Use precise language and domain-specific vocabulary to inform about or explain the topic.

Informative Text

W.8.2e **Establish and Maintain a Formal Style**
- Establish and maintain a formal style.

W.8.2f **Provide a Conclusion**
- Provide a conclusion that follows from and supports the information or explanation presented.

Analyze and Prewrite

Conduct Research

Informative/explanatory texts are also called expository texts. This type of writing examines and expresses ideas, concepts, and information. A research report is a type of informative/explanatory text that you may be familiar with. When writing a research report, you do research on a topic and evaluate the information that you find. You may also state your opinion on the topic and back up your opinion with evidence from outside sources.

Writers often choose their topics by thinking about their interests. They might ask themselves, "Who or what would I like to know more about?" Writers also consider what resources are available and then refocus the research topic so that it is neither too broad nor too narrow. For example, if only one or two sources exist on a topic, a writer may not find enough information about it. In this case the writer should broaden the research topic so more resources are available. On the other hand, if a huge number of sources are available, the writer may have trouble sorting through them all. In that case the writer should narrow the research topic so fewer resources are available.

Once a writer chooses a topic, he or she often generates one major question about the topic to answer in the report. For example, if you were to write a report about Rosa Parks, your research question might be, "How did the actions of Rosa Parks help advance the civil rights movement?" If you were to begin your research with this major research question, your research findings would make you think about additional questions that you need to answer, and your research would continue. Depending on what new questions you generate, your research might take you along multiple avenues of investigation.

As writers do research on their topics, they gather relevant information from multiple print and digital sources. **Relevant information** addresses the major question that you want to answer in your report. Types of relevant information include well-chosen facts, definitions, concrete details, quotations, examples, and other information related to the topic.

Writers always assess, or judge, the credibility and accuracy of each source. A **credible source** presents current, or up-to-date, information on the topic and is written by an authority or expert in the field. A credible source presents information objectively, without a hidden agenda, and cites sources to back up information. An **accurate source** presents information that is true. To determine if a source is accurate, you might verify the information in another source.

LEARN FROM THE MODEL

Skim the student model about Franklin D. Roosevelt on pages 734–735 of *Glencoe Literature* to find out what research methods the writer may have used.

1. What is the topic of this report? What major research question might the writer have used to help focus the report?

_____

_____

_____

_____

2. Look again at page 735 of *Glencoe Literature.* Notice the Works Cited list at the bottom of the report. How can you tell that the writer used both print and digital sources?

_____

_____

_____

_____

3. Now look at the last entry of the Works Cited list. Do you think this source is credible and accurate and contains relevant information? Explain your answer.

_____

_____

_____

_____

Informative Text

4. What other types of credible and accurate sources might the writer have used to gather relevant information for this report? Explain.

_____

_____

_____

_____

_____

APPLY WHAT YOU'VE LEARNED

W.8.2a
W.8.6
W.8.7
W.8.8

5. What topic will your research report be about? Remember that your topic shouldn't be too narrow or too broad.

_____

_____

_____

6. Use that topic to generate your major research question. Write it below.

_____

_____

_____

_____

7. When doing digital card catalog or Internet searches, you need to use effective search terms to narrow your findings. What search terms will you use to locate information about your topic? List at least five search terms on the lines below. Then revise those terms if they are too narrow or too broad.

_____

_____

_____

_____

_____

8. What credible print and digital sources contain information about your topic? List at least five possible print and digital sources on the lines below. How do you know the information in these sources will be relevant and accurate? Explain.

_____

_____

_____

_____

_____

_____

Peer or Adult Review Discuss your research plans with a classmate or an adult, or e-mail him or her your plans. Ask for ideas on how to improve your topic, research question, and possible sources. Evaluate the suggestions you receive and then revise what you've written or try a new approach.

Develop a Topic

Good writers of informative/explanatory texts choose topics that are interesting. To develop their topics, good writers include relevant well-chosen facts, definitions, concrete details, quotations, examples, or other information.

LEARN FROM THE MODEL

Reread the student model on pages 734–735 of *Glencoe Literature* to see how the writer develops the topic throughout the report.

1. How does the writer introduce the topic in the report? In paragraphs 1 and 2, how does the writer provide a preview of the information that follows in the rest of the report?

_____

_____

_____

_____

_____

Informative Text

2. Reread the first paragraph of the student model. What is the **thesis**, or controlling idea, of the report?

_____

_____

_____

_____

3. What facts, definitions, concrete details, quotations, examples, and other relevant information does the writer use to develop and support the thesis? Find examples of each type of information used in the student model. Record your answers in the chart. The first row is done as an example for you.

Relevant Information	Text	Paragraph
Fact	Roosevelt is the only U.S. president elected to four terms.	1
Definition		
Concrete Detail		
Quotation		
Example		
Other Information		

Informative Text

4. Writers organize ideas, concepts, and information into broader categories. Arranging the information into broader categories helps writers to structure their reports. Writers examine the information they have collected in their research, looking for common elements that will help them categorize the information. Then they use the categories to guide them as they write.

Reread each paragraph of the student model on pages 734–735 to find out how the writer organizes the ideas and information about Roosevelt into broader categories. Paragraphs 2–5 basically cover two broader categories. Below, write what each category is and provide some examples from the text of the information that falls under each category.

Category 1: _____

_____

_____

_____

Category 2: _____

_____

_____

_____

5. To help readers understand informative/explanatory texts, writers often include

- graphics, such as images, maps, and charts
- formatting, such as heads and subheads
- multimedia elements, such as URLs for video clips

Which of these elements could the writer have used in the report about Roosevelt? Explain how these elements could have improved the report.

_____

_____

_____

_____

_____

Informative Text

W.8.2, a,b
W.8.7
W.8.8

APPLY WHAT YOU'VE LEARNED

6. As you conduct research on your topic, you should use what you learn from each source to generate additional related questions for further research and investigation. On the lines below, write three focused questions that you will answer through further research. Explain how these additional questions allow for multiple avenues of exploration.

_____

_____

_____

_____

_____

_____

_____

7. As you research, take notes on note cards and record source information on source cards. Be sure to quote or paraphrase the information and conclusions found in your resources. Then use your notes to create an outline. Your outline will help you organize information about your topic into paragraphs.

Each paragraph should include a main point related to your topic and support for that point. The support may include the relevant, well-chosen facts, definitions, concrete details, quotations, examples, or other information on your note cards. (See pages R15–R16 in the Writing Handbook of **Glencoe Literature** for more help with taking notes on notes cards, creating source cards, and writing an outline.)

Topic: _____

Thesis: _____

I. _____

    A. _____

    B. _____

    C. _____

Informative Text

II. _____
   A. _____
   B. _____
   C. _____

III. _____
   A. _____
   B. _____
   C. _____

IV. _____
   A. _____
   B. _____
   C. _____

8. What formatting, such as heads and subheads; graphics, such as charts, maps, or photos; and multimedia elements, such as URLs for video clips; will you use in your report? Explain how these elements will help readers understand your text.

_____
_____
_____
_____
_____
_____

W.8.5
W.8.6
Peer or Adult Review Discuss your outline and ideas for formatting, graphics, and multimedia with a classmate or an adult, or e-mail them to your reviewer. Ask for ideas on how to improve the outline and ideas for formatting, graphics, and multimedia. Evaluate any suggestions you receive and then revise what you've written or try a new approach.

Informative Text

Use Transitions and Precise Language

Good writers create **cohesive** texts. In a cohesive text, the ideas in sentences and paragraphs are organized logically and linked clearly so the reader understands how each new paragraph relates to the topic and thesis. Writers use transitions to link the ideas in sentences and paragraphs. **Transitions** are words, phrases, and clauses that help clarify the relationships among ideas and concepts. Examples of transitional words and phrases that are useful in expository writing include *in addition, however, after that,* and *more importantly.*

Good writers also use precise language and domain-specific vocabulary, or vocabulary that is specific to the topic of the report, in order to give the reader more detailed information and explanations. For example, if you were writing a report about a scientific topic, such as the environment, you would want to use vocabulary specific to the topic, such as *ecosystem, invasive species*, and *extinction.* These words are the most precise choices for the context.

LEARN FROM THE MODEL

Analyze how the writer of the student model on pages 734–735 of **Glencoe Literature** uses transitions and precise language.

1. What transitional word does the writer of the student model use to link paragraphs 4 and 5? What purpose does this transition serve?

_____

_____

_____

_____

2. Reread paragraph 2 of the student model. Identify three examples of precise language and domain-specific vocabulary that relate to information about Roosevelt. How does this language help clarify the writer's main point in the paragraph?

_____

_____

_____

_____

_____

_____

_____

_____

APPLY WHAT YOU'VE LEARNED

3. Review your outline on pages 160–161. What words, phrases, or clauses would help connect the ideas from one paragraph to the next? Write down three possible transitions below.

_____

_____

_____

_____

_____

4. What precise language related to your topic can you use to clarify your main points? What domain-specific vocabulary will you use? List a few examples on the lines below.

_____

_____

_____

_____

Informative Text

5. Pick one main point from your outline. Write a few sentences using appropriate and varied transitions to link this point to its support, such as facts, details, or quotations. Include at least one example of precise language or domain-specific language in the sentences to help the reader understand the topic.

_____

_____

_____

_____

_____

_____

_____

W.8.5
W.8.6 **Peer or Adult Review** Discuss your ideas for transitions, precise language, and domain-specific vocabulary with a classmate or an adult in person or through e-mail. Ask for suggestions on other transitions and language that might help to create a more cohesive report. Evaluate the suggestions you receive and then revise what you've written or try a new approach.

Establish and Maintain a Formal Style

In expository writing, it is important for writers to use a formal style and to maintain that style throughout the report. In **formal writing,** you write from the third-person point of view and you avoid using conversational language, slang, and contractions. Writers using a formal style should also use an objective **tone,** or attitude, so readers think the report is reasonable and unbiased, or fair. For example, if a writer is presenting information about water pollution, the writer should not include a statement such as, "I think factories shouldn't dump waste into water because that's just gross and who wants to drink that?" The tone of the statement is subjective (it reflects the writer's personal opinion) and is presented too casually. The writer would sound more credible if he or she presented objective facts about the negative impact such pollution has on a water supply.

Informative Text

LEARN FROM THE MODEL

Analyze how the writer of the student model on pages 734–735 of **Glencoe Literature** establishes and maintains a formal style and tone.

1. In the student model, what words and phrases help create a formal style? Find two examples and write them in the following chart. Explain how each example makes the style more formal.

Word or Phrase	How It Makes the Style Formal

2. How would you describe the writer's tone, or attitude, in the student model? Support your answer with evidence from the text.

_____

_____

_____

_____

_____

_____

Informative Text

W.8.2e **APPLY WHAT YOU'VE LEARNED**

3. Look at your outline on pages 160–161. Choose one paragraph to develop on the lines below. Focus on establishing and maintaining a formal style and an objective tone as you write.

_____

_____

_____

_____

_____

_____

_____

_____

_____

_____

_____

W.8.5
W.8.6 **Peer or Adult Review** Give a copy of your paragraph or e-mail the text to a classmate or an adult. Ask for suggestions on how improve your formal style and tone. Evaluate any suggestions you receive and then revise what you've written or try a new approach.

Provide a Conclusion

An effective informative/explanatory text ends with a strong conclusion. The conclusion should follow from and support the information or explanation presented in earlier paragraphs. A strong conclusion links back to the writer's main points about the topic. The conclusion allows the writer to make a final impression by including a comment that ties the text to a bigger idea.

LEARN FROM THE MODEL

Analyze how the writer of the student model on pages 734–735 of *Glencoe Literature* builds a strong conclusion.

1. Reread the last paragraph of the student model. How does this conclusion support the information that the writer presented in earlier paragraphs?

_____

_____

_____

_____

_____

2. What final thought does the writer leave with the reader? Is this an effective concluding statement? Why or why not?

_____

_____

_____

_____

_____

W.8.2f APPLY WHAT YOU'VE LEARNED

3. On the lines below, write down possible ideas for the conclusion of your report. How will the conclusion link back to your earlier points in the report? What final thought might you leave with the reader?

_____

_____

_____

_____

_____

_____

_____

Informative Text

W.8.5
W.8.6

Peer or Adult Review Discuss your ideas for an effective conclusion with a classmate or an adult in person or through e-mail. Ask for suggestions on how to create a stronger link back to the points in your report for a more lasting final impression. Evaluate any suggestions you receive and then revise what you've written or try a new approach.

Draft

W.8.6
W.8.10

Before you begin drafting, review your prewriting notes on pages 155–167. Then use a computer to write your first draft, following the instructions below.

Write the Introduction

W.8.2a, e

Begin by writing the introductory paragraph of your research report. Your introduction should

- grab the reader's attention (consider starting with an anecdote, a surprising fact or detail, a well-chosen quotation, or a thought-provoking question)
- tell what your report is about, previewing what is to follow
- present your thesis statement, or controlling idea
- establish a formal style and an objective tone

Write the Body

W.8.2a–e
W.8.4
W.8.7
W.8.8
L.8.6

Write Cohesive Paragraphs Use your outline as a guide when you write the body, or main paragraphs, of your report. Begin each paragraph with a topic sentence that expresses the main point of the paragraph. Next, think about your audience and what they may or may not know about that point. Then support the point with information from multiple sources. You might include relevant facts, definitions, concrete details, quotations, examples, or other information that you wrote on your note cards. Only include support that will guide and inform your readers' understanding of your point. As you write, remember to organize your ideas, concepts, and information into broader categories.

Use Transitions and Precise Language Use a variety of transitions to create cohesion and to clarify the relationships between the ideas from one sentence or paragraph to the next. Remember to use precise language and domain-specific vocabulary that is specific to your topic. For example, if you are writing about the heart and the circulatory system, you will want to use words that are specific to the circulatory system, such as *veins, arteries,* and *ventricles.*

Use Formatting, Graphics, and Multimedia As you write, remember to include formatting (such as heads and subheads), when appropriate, to help guide your readers. Consider including graphics (such as tables, maps, or graphs) and/ or multimedia elements (such as URLs for video clips) if they will help readers comprehend your topic.

Credit Your Sources As you write, maintain the formal style and objective tone that you established in the introduction. Avoid plagiarizing, or presenting an author's words or ideas as if they are your own. You must credit your sources for material directly quoted and also for any facts or ideas paraphrased from the source. You should give the source information in footnotes or in parentheses at the end of the sentence where the information appears. Also include a Bibliography or Works Cited list at the end of your report. See pages R16–R17 of the Writing Handbook in *Glencoe Literature* for more help.

Write the Conclusion

W.8.2f Finally, write the conclusion of your report. Make sure it follows from and supports the information or explanation you presented in your report. The conclusion should restate your thesis statement in a different way and summarize the main points in the report. You should end with a strong closing statement that leaves a lasting impression and ties the text to a bigger idea.

Revise

W.8.4 To revise your research report, you will focus on the content, or message, of your writing. You will apply one or more of these four revision strategies:

- **Add** details and information to make the message clearer.
- **Remove** distracting or unnecessary words or ideas.
- **Replace** boring or overused words with precise language.
- **Rearrange** phrases and sentences to be sure information is presented logically.

The questions that follow will show you how to use these revision strategies. They will help you consider whether the development, organization, and style of your report are appropriate to your task, purpose, and audience.

Informative Text

Focus and Coherence

W.8.4 Ask yourself each of the following questions. Then evaluate your report. When you can answer "yes" to each question, check the box before the question.

☐ Does my report have a clear focus?

☐ Do all the parts work together so that I achieve my purpose?

Organization

W.8.2a, f Ask yourself each of the following questions. Then evaluate your report. When you can answer "yes" to each question, check the box before the question.

☐ Does the beginning clearly introduce my topic?

☐ Does the body, or main paragraphs, organize ideas, concepts, and information into broader categories?

☐ Does the conclusion follow from the information or explanation I presented in the report?

Development of Ideas

W.8.2b Ask yourself each of the following questions. Then evaluate your report. When you can answer "yes" to each question, check the box before the question.

☐ Does my report develop ideas in a logical order?

☐ Do I develop the topic with relevant, well-chosen facts, definitions, concrete details, quotations, examples, or other information that is suitable to what my audience may or may not know about the topic?

☐ Do I include formatting, graphics, or multimedia that help the reader understand the text?

Voice—Word Choice

W.8.2d, e
L.8.3 Ask yourself each of the following questions. Then evaluate your report. When you can answer "yes" to each question, check the box before the question.

☐ Do I use precise language and domain-specific vocabulary?

☐ Do I use knowledge of language to maintain consistency in style?

☐ Do I establish and maintain a formal style and an objective tone?

Informative Text

Voice—Sentence Fluency

Ask yourself each of the following questions. Then evaluate your report. When you can answer "yes" to each question, check the box before the question.

☐ Does my writing flow smoothly?

☐ Do I use a variety of sentence patterns for interest, meaning, and style?

☐ Does my report include a variety of transitions to link sentences and paragraphs, create cohesion, and clarify the relationships among ideas and concepts?

☐ Do I emphasize important points?

W.8.5 W.8.6

Peer or Adult Review Share your report and the checklists with a classmate or an adult. Have your reviewer use the checklists to evaluate your report and offer suggestions for improvement. You might then e-mail specific questions or responses that you have in response to their comments. Next, revise your report, as needed, possibly trying a new approach to cover areas of concern.

Edit and Proofread

Correct Errors in Grammar

Editing involves correcting errors in grammar, usage, mechanics, and spelling. Begin the editing stage by taking a careful look at your sentences. Make sure that each sentence expresses a complete thought in a way that is grammatically correct. Use the checklist below to edit your sentences.

SENTENCE-EDITING CHECKLIST

☐ Have I avoided sentence fragments?

☐ Have I avoided run-on sentences?

☐ Do verbs agree with their subjects?

☐ Are verbs used correctly?

☐ Are pronouns in the proper case and used correctly?

☐ Do pronouns have clear antecedents?

☐ Have I avoided misplaced and dangling modifiers?

☐ Have I used phrases and clauses correctly?

☐ Have I used active and passive voice correctly?

Informative Text

Correct Errors in Mechanics and Spelling

**L.8.1
L.8.2, a, b** Next, proofread for and correct any errors in mechanics (punctuation and capitalization) and spelling. Use the checklist below to edit your report for mechanics and spelling. You should also use a dictionary to check and confirm spellings.

PROOFREADING CHECKLIST

☐ Are punctuation marks used as needed, such as using commas, ellipses, and dashes to indicate a pause or break?

☐ Are all words spelled correctly?

☐ Are capital letters used as needed?

**W.8.5
W.8.6** **Peer or Adult Review** Share your report and the editing-and-proofreading checklists with a classmate or an adult. Have your reviewer use the checklists to evaluate your report and offer suggestions for improvement. Discuss the suggestions in person or e-mail specific questions or responses to their comments. Then use a computer to write the final draft of your report.

Present/Publish

W.8.6 After you have written and polished your research report, you will want to publish and present it so classmates, friends, and family can respond to it. You may wish to consider some of these publishing and presenting options:

- Create a class collection of research reports.
- Enter your report into a writing contest.
- Post your report on your school or class Web site.
- Publish your report on the Internet, with the help of an adult.

Consider using technology, including the Internet, to publish your report. Take advantage of the flexibility of technology, which allows you to type in text, move it around, make changes, and create a clear, logical display. Also consider how you can use technology to interact and collaborate with others. You may wish to consult some of the projects in the Reading section of this book for additional publishing ideas that include technology.

Grammar Practice

L.8.1b **Active and Passive Voice**

Sentences can be written with their verbs in the active voice or the passive voice. When the subject performs the action of the verb, the verb is in the active voice. When the subject receives the action of the verb, the verb is in the passive voice. Of course, this means that the subject is different in each voice, even if the sentences are saying basically the same thing.

Active Voice: I wrote a research report.

Passive Voice: A research report was written by me.

L.8.3a **Using the Active Voice**

The active voice is usually a stronger and more direct way to express an idea. It is clear, and it is almost always a shorter way to say something than it is to use the passive voice. This is because the passive voice requires a helping verb—a form of *be*—and the past participle. Because the active voice tends to be stronger, you should use it for most of your writing.

EXERCISE A: USING THE ACTIVE VOICE

Each sentence below is in the passive voice. Rewrite each one so that it is in the active voice.

1. Society was affected by the presidency of Franklin D. Roosevelt.

_____

2. Congress was persuaded by FDR to help Britain defend democracy.

_____

3. The liberation of Europe was begun by the Battle of Normandy.

_____

Informative Text

Using the Passive Voice

L.8.3a Sometimes it makes more sense to use passive voice in a sentence. If you want to put emphasis on the receiver of the action or you don't know who performed the action, the passive voice is often the better voice to use. The following examples are both cases in which the passive voice works better than the active voice would.

Examples: Peace was restored but only after FDR's death.

Objections to American involvement in the war were raised.

EXERCISE B: USING THE PASSIVE VOICE

Each sentence below is in the active voice. Rewrite each one so that it is in the passive voice.

4. The Great Depression harmed the United States.

_____

5. Some people designed the New Deal to help the country recover.

_____

6. On D-Day, enemy soldiers killed many Allied soldiers.

_____

Deciding Which Voice to Use

L.8.1d As stated earlier, it is usually better to use the active voice, but it is sometimes desirable to use the passive voice. One general rule to follow is to use the active voice unless you have a good reason to use the passive voice instead.

One rule you must follow is to stick with the voice you've chosen for a sentence.

Correct: The Japanese attacked Pearl Harbor and destroyed many ships.

Incorrect: The Japanese attacked Pearl Harbor, and many ships were destroyed.

L.8.1b
L.8.3a

EXERCISE C: USING ACTIVE AND PASSIVE VOICE

Rewrite each sentence, changing the verb from active to passive or from passive to active.

7. Someone wrote the Student Model about President Franklin D. Roosevelt.

_____

_____

8. Our reports were assigned by Ms. Waters.

_____

_____

9. The subject of my report, César Chavez, was chosen by me.

_____

_____

10. The United Farm Workers was begun by Chavez.

_____

_____

W.8.1d **Check Your Writing** Read through your research report to make sure that you have mostly used the active voice. Check that you have used the passive voice only when it is appropriate and a better choice than the active voice. Remember that the passive voice should, in general, be avoided because the active voice tends to be stronger. Correct any inappropriate shifts in verb voice.

Informative Text

Grammar Practice

L.8.2a

Commas, Ellipses, and Dashes to Indicate a Pause or Break

It is often necessary or desirable to indicate a pause or other break in a sentence. Inserting commas is one way to do this, but commas are not always the best means of indicating a break. Parentheses (( )) can also be used for this purpose, and so can dashes (—) and ellipsis points (. . .) under certain conditions.

Commas

Commas can be used to set off a word, a phrase, or a clause if the information enclosed by them is not essential to the meaning of a sentence.

Examples: Franklin Delano Roosevelt, though wealthy, cared about the mass unemployment.

Few people realized that FDR, a victim of polio, was disabled.

Franklin Delano Roosevelt, who died while in office, introduced work programs.

Dashes

A dash is a horizontal line that is longer than a hyphen. If you are using a typewriter, a dash is indicated by two hyphens right next to each other (--). This form is also acceptable if you are using a computer, although there are ways to make your word processing program provide an actual dash.

Like commas and parentheses, dashes can also be used to set off material. Dashes, however, emphasize the set-off text or indicate an abrupt break in thought. Depending on where the enclosed material appears, one dash or two may be used.

Examples: FDR ran successfully for office—the fourth time he'd run!

FDR's run for the presidency—for his fourth term!—was successful.

His war actions are generally thought well of today—except for his agreeing to put U.S. citizens of Japanese descent in special camps—although many people disagree with Truman's actions after FDR's death.

Dashes (like parentheses) allow set-off material to be punctuated without confusing the reader.

Example: As president, FDR was loved by many—and his wife, Eleanor, by even more— though he was also disliked by some.

EXERCISE A: USING COMMAS AND DASHES TO INDICATE A PAUSE OR BREAK

Insert a caret (^) in each place in the sentence where punctuation is needed to indicate a pause or a break. Then, on the line on the left, write **C** for commas or **D** for dashes to indicate the kind of punctuation that would be better to use.

___**1.** The United States in the years of FDR's presidency rose to a place of importance in the world.

___**2.** The writer who clearly cited several varied, impressive works in the report obviously did in-depth research on the subject.

___**3.** The report was interesting I really enjoyed reading it as well as informative.

ELLIPSIS POINTS

L.8.2b Ellipsis points are three dots (periods), separated by spaces. Their main purpose is to show that a word or words have been omitted from a quotation without changing its essential meaning. For example:

In his first inaugural address, FDR said, "So first of all, let me assert . . . that the only thing we have to fear is fear itself . . . In every dark hour of our national life a leadership of frankness and vigor has met with that understanding and support of the people themselves which is essential to victory."

Ellipsis points are sometimes used at the end of a sentence to show that the writer (or the person speaking in dialogue) has trailed off without completing his or her thought. For example:

I don't know what topic to choose. I just don't know . . .

Informative Text

EXERCISE B: USING ELLIPSES TO INDICATE A BREAK OR OMISSION

Put brackets ([]) around one or more sections from each of the following sentences in the student model that could be omitted and replaced with ellipsis points, without changing the basic meaning of the original. Be sure that the text that is left after the ellipsis points still reads as a complete sentence.

4. Roosevelt, commonly known as FDR, is the only U.S. president elected to four terms (*Britannica*), which included major challenges at home and abroad.

5. Even his biggest opponent in Congress, Senator Robert Taft, had to acknowledge FDR's impact on the world: "The President's death removes the greatest figure of our time . . ."

L.8.2a, b | **Check Your Writing** Read through your research report to check it for the use of commas and dashes that indicate a pause or break. Also look for any places where you used ellipsis points to indicate a break or omission. Make sure that you have used commas, dashes, and ellipsis points correctly throughout your paper.

Informative Text

Writing Workshop
NARRATIVE
Glencoe Literature Connection: Raymond's Run, pages 13–28

Before starting the lesson, read the following selection and complete the lesson activities in **Glencoe Literature.**

"Raymond's Run" by Toni Cade Bambara **(pages 13–28)**

RL.8.10
W.8.3
W.8.9, a
W.8.10

In this lesson, you will study Toni Cade Bambara's short story "Raymond's Run" to discover how the author effectively uses the narrative writing methods and techniques listed below. You will then use these methods and techniques to write your own narrative. As you complete this workshop, you will practice the following standards:

W.8.3a | **Engage and Orient the Reader**
- Establish a context.
- Establish a point of view.
- Introduce a narrator and/or characters.

W.8.3a, c | **Sequence Events**
- Organize an event sequence that unfolds naturally and logically.
- Use a variety of transition words, phrases, and clauses to convey sequence, signal shifts from one time frame or setting to another, and show the relationships among experiences and events.

W.8.3b, d | **Use Narrative Techniques**
- Use techniques such as dialogue, pacing, description, and reflection, to develop experiences, events, and/or characters.
- Use precise words and phrases, relevant descriptive details, and sensory language to capture the action and convey experiences and events.

W.8.3e | **Provide a Conclusion**
- Provide a conclusion that follows from and reflects on the narrated experiences or events.

Narrative

Analyze and Prewrite

Engage and Orient the Reader

Narrative writing tells a story that is either fictional, as in a short story, or true, as in an autobiography or a biography. Good narrative writers engage and orient the reader by setting a context (such as the setting and situation), establishing a point of view, and introducing a narrator and/or main characters. In a short story, the context often relates to a problem that involves the main character, and the story can be told from a variety of points of view.

LEARN FROM THE MODEL

Reread the opening paragraphs on pages 15–16 of *Glencoe Literature* to see how Toni Cade Bambara engages and orients the reader in "Raymond's Run."

1. What context (setting, situation, problem) does the narrator set out on pages 15–16?

_____

_____

_____

2. Use the chart below to describe the narrator of the story.

Characteristic	Description of Narrator
Age	
Gender	
Appearance	
Feelings	

Narrative

3. What point of view does Bambara use in this story? Is the narrator a character in the story, or does the narrator tell events from outside the story?

_____

_____

_____

4. How would you describe the narrator's attitude on these pages? Support your response with at least two examples from the text.

_____

_____

_____

_____

W.8.3a   **APPLY WHAT YOU'VE LEARNED**

5. Establish a context for your narrative. What setting will your story take place in? What situation will you establish?

_____

_____

_____

6. What point of view will work best for your story? Will the narrator be a character in the story, or will the narrator tell events from outside the story? Explain your choice.

_____

_____

_____

_____

_____

Narrative

7. How will you establish the plot of your story? Which characters will help set up the events?

_____

_____

_____

W.8.5
W.8.6

Peer or Adult Review Discuss your story ideas with a classmate or an adult, or e-mail him or her your ideas. Ask for suggestions on how to improve your setting, plot, and characters. Then revise what you've written or try a new approach.

Organize an Event Sequence and Provide a Conclusion

Narrative writers organize the events of the plot so that they unfold naturally and logically. Each event builds on the one before to create a sequence of events that is believable to readers and tells a complete story. Good narrative writers use a variety of transitions to convey sequence (*first, next, then*), signal shifts from one time frame or setting to another (*before that, once long ago, over there*), and show the relationships among experiences and events (*because, as a result, after all*). They also provide a conclusion that follows from and reflects on the narrated experiences or events.

LEARN FROM THE MODEL

The ending of "Raymond's Run" reveals a change in the narrator's attitude and what she truly values. This conclusion reflects the narrated events of the story. The author has carefully sequenced the story to lead to this conclusion. Review the order of events and the ending in "Raymond's Run" to see how the author creates a coherent sequence of events and conclusion.

1. Which events in the story serve to set up the ending? How do these events unfold naturally and logically?

_____

_____

_____

_____

_____

_____

Narrative

2. An effective conclusion to a story reflects the narrated events. Sometimes a conclusion includes an important change that a character goes through. Do you think the conclusion of "Raymond's Run" is effective? Why or why not?

_____

_____

_____

_____

3. What transition words, phrases, and clauses does Bambara use in "Raymond's Run"? Remember that transitions help clarify the sequence of events, shifts in time or setting, and relationships between events or ideas. Fill in the chart below with two examples of each type, underlining the transitional words, phrases, or clauses. One example has been done for you.

Transitional Words, Phrases, and Clauses	Examples	Page Numbers
To show sequence	<u>Then</u> they all look at Raymond who has just . . .	19
To signal shifts in time frame or setting		
To show relationships among experiences and ideas		

Narrative

W.8.3a, c, e **APPLY WHAT YOU'VE LEARNED**

4. What will be the sequence of events in your story? Use as many boxes as you need.

Event:

↓

Event:

↓

Event:

↓

Event:

↓

Event:

↓

Event:

Narrative

5. How will you organize this sequence of events so that it unfolds naturally and logically?

_____

_____

_____

_____

6. What transitional words, phrases and clauses will you use to show sequence, and to signal shifts from one time frame or setting to another? What transitions will you use to show the relationships among experiences and events?

_____

_____

_____

_____

_____

7. How will the conclusion of your narrative reflect on the events in your narrative?

_____

_____

_____

_____

_____

W.8.5
W.8.6
Peer or Adult Review Discuss your story ideas with a classmate or an adult, or e-mail him or her your ideas. Ask for ideas on how to improve your setting, plot, and characters. Then revise what you've written or try a new approach.

Narrative

Use Narrative Techniques: Description

Description is a detailed portrayal of a person, place, or thing. Good writers use elements of description to convey a vivid picture of the setting, experiences, events, and characters in a story. These elements include

- precise words and phrases
- sensory language, or details that appeal to the five senses—touch, smell, sound, sight, and taste
- a variety of verbs (for example, active and passive voice, conditional and subjunctive moods) to achieve particular effects
- telling details, or concise and thoughtful particulars that tell the reader something important

LEARN FROM THE MODEL

Reread passages from "Raymond's Run" of *Glencoe Literature* as indicated below and analyze how Bambara uses elements of description.

1. On page 17, what words, phrases, and details does Bambara use to present the setting of Squeaky's neighborhood and to convey the narrator's attitude? Explain.

   _____

   _____

   _____

   _____

   _____

2. Reread the last paragraph on page 21 and read to the paragraph's end on page 22. What sensory details does Bambara include and to what senses do they appeal? What kind of mood do these details help create?

   _____

   _____

   _____

   _____

   _____

Narrative

W.8.3b, d
L.8.3, a

APPLY WHAT YOU'VE LEARNED

3. Write sentences in which you describe and elaborate on how characters think, act, feel, and interact at each point in your narrative. Refer to "Raymond's Run" in *Glencoe Literature* for ideas and techniques. Be sure to include

- precise words and phrases
- sensory language, or details that appeal to the five senses—touch, smell, sound, sight, and taste
- a variety of verbs (active and passive voice, conditional and subjunctive moods) to achieve particular effects
- telling details, or concise and thoughtful particulars that tell the reader something important

Refer to your sequence of events graphic organizer on page 184 as needed.

Event/Situation:

_____

_____

_____

Interactions and Reactions of Those Involved:

_____

_____

_____

Event/Situation:

_____

_____

_____

Interactions and Reactions of Those Involved:

_____

_____

_____

Narrative

W.8.5
W.8.6

Peer or Adult Review Discuss your narrative ideas with a classmate or an adult, or e-mail him or her your ideas. Ask for suggestions on how to improve your setting, plot, and characters. Then revise what you've written or try a new approach.

Use Narrative Techniques: Dialogue and Pacing

Dialogue is the conversation between characters in a literary work. In a narrative, dialogue brings to life the qualities and personalities of the characters by showing what they are thinking and feeling as they react to others and to events. Dialogue can help create mood and develop theme. Dialogue also advances a story's **plot**, or sequence of events, and is therefore a key element in a story's **pacing**, or the speed with which the action proceeds.

LEARN FROM THE MODEL

Reread passages from "Raymond's Run" in *Glencoe Literature* as indicated below and analyze how Bambara uses dialogue and pacing.

1. Read Rosie's line of dialogue in the third paragraph on page 19. How does this dialogue add to the conflict?

_____

_____

_____

_____

_____

2. Reread the rest of the dialogue between Squeaky and the other girls on page 19. How does this dialogue bring to life Squeaky's personality?

_____

_____

_____

_____

_____

Narrative

3. The story begins not long before a big race for Squeaky, and it ends immediately following the announcement of the race's winner. How does Bambara use elements such as dialogue, plot events, and time shifts to pace the story?

_____

_____

_____

_____

W.8.3b | **APPLY WHAT YOU'VE LEARNED**

4. Review your sentences on page 187 in which you wrote descriptions of events, situations, and characters in your narrative. Write down key sections or parts of dialogue to show what those characters are thinking and feeling as they react to others and to events and situations. Add information about how you plan to use pacing to develop your story. Refer to "Raymond's Run" for ideas and techniques. Refer to your sequence of events graphic organizer on page 184 as needed.

_____

_____

_____

_____

_____

_____

_____

W.8.5 **W.8.6** | **Peer or Adult Review** Discuss your narrative ideas with a classmate or an adult, or e-mail him or her your ideas. Ask for suggestions on how to improve your setting, plot, and characters. Then revise what you've written or try a new approach.

Narrative

Use Narrative Techniques: Reflection

Reflection is the inclusion of the thoughts, opinions, or attitudes of the narrator or of other characters. Reflection can be included in dialogue or in descriptive or explanatory passages. Reflection is used to develop experiences, events, and characters in a narrative.

LEARN FROM THE MODEL

Reread passages from "Raymond's Run" in **Glencoe Literature** as indicated below and analyze how Bambara includes reflection.

1. When Squeaky shares her thoughts, feelings, and opinions, a reader can form a clearer picture of what her personality is like. For example, read the passage on page 16 where Squeaky describes her father beating her in a race, and she calls that "private information." Her sharing of this information not only helps the reader understand how prideful she is about her running, it also helps develop the plot by showing how important the big race is to her. Find an example of another passage that has a similar effect. What larger comment about Squeaky's personality and values is Bambara making in that passage?

   _____

   _____

   _____

   _____

   _____

2. Read the last full paragraph of the story, starting on page 25 and continuing on page 26. People think Squeaky is excited because of the race results. Based on Squeaky's reflections in this paragraph, are those people right? How do Squeaky's reflections reveal a development in her personality, and how do they provide a satisfying resolution to the plot?

   _____

   _____

   _____

   _____

Narrative

W.8.3b **APPLY WHAT YOU'VE LEARNED**

3. Write notes about the reflections that the characters have experienced, observed, or resolved in the events of your narrative. Write notes showing how you will include reflection in dialogue, in your description of characters' unspoken thoughts, or in the narrator's commentary. Then explain how you will use reflection to develop the characters and the plot.

_____

_____

_____

_____

_____

_____

_____

_____

_____

_____

W.8.5
W.8.6 **Peer or Adult Review** Discuss your narrative ideas with a classmate or an adult, or e-mail him or her your ideas. Ask for suggestions on how to improve your setting, plot, and characters. Then revise what you've written or try a new approach.

Narrative

Draft

<table>
<tr><td>W.8.6
W.8.10</td><td>Before you begin drafting, review your prewriting notes on pages 180–191. Then use the instructions that follow to write your first draft on a computer.</td></tr>
</table>

<table>
<tr><td>W.8.3a, b</td><td></td></tr>
</table>

Write the Opening

Begin by writing the opening to your narrative. In the opening, you should establish the context, or the setting and the situation, and the characters who are involved. You should also establish the point of view.

In your opening, add the descriptive details about the characters and events from your prewriting notes.

<table>
<tr><td>W.8.3b</td><td></td></tr>
</table>

Include Dialogue

As you write, include dialogue to help flesh out the characters and events, enhance the pacing, and move the plot along. Identify the purpose of the dialogue and the type of language you will use to convey each character's age, background, and personality. You will also want to communicate each character's thoughts and feelings.

Use tag lines (the words that identify the speaker, such as "said Isabella") to identify each speaker. Avoid using *said* repeatedly in tag lines, and instead use a variety of descriptive words, such as *answered, asked, replied, screamed, shouted, murmured,* or *whispered.*

<table>
<tr><td>W.8.3b, c, d</td><td></td></tr>
</table>

Write the Body

Next, use your prewriting notes to write the body, or main part, of your narrative. Remember to

- use descriptive details to develop characters and events
- pace the sequence of events you have mapped out so that events build on one another and unfold naturally and logically
- use a variety of transition words, phrases, and clauses to convey sequence, signal shifts from one time frame or setting to another, and show the relationships among experiences and events
- use narrative techniques, such as dialogue, pacing, description, and reflection to develop experiences, events, and/or characters
- use precise words and phrases, telling details, and sensory language to capture the action and convey experiences and events.

<table>
<tr><td>W.8.3e</td><td></td></tr>
</table>

Write the Conclusion

Finally, write the conclusion, or ending, of your narrative. Make sure that your conclusion follows from and reflects on narrated experiences or events.

Narrative

Revise

W.8.4
W.8.5
L.8.3

To revise your narrative, you will focus on the content, or the message, of your writing and apply one or more of these four revision strategies:

- **add** details and information to make the message clearer
- **remove** distracting or unnecessary words or ideas
- **substitute** more precise or stronger words for bland or overused language
- **rearrange** phrases and sentences to be sure the message is logically presented

The questions that follow will show you how to use these revision strategies. They will help you consider whether the development, organization, and style of your narrative are appropriate to task, purpose, and audience.

W.8.3a
W.8.4

Focus and Coherence

Ask yourself the following questions. Then evaluate your narrative and check each box when you can answer "yes" to the question.

☐ Does my narrative have a clear focus?

☐ Do all the parts work together so that I achieve my purpose?

☐ Will readers be able to follow the sequence of events?

W.8.3a, c, e

Organization

Ask yourself the following questions. Then evaluate your narrative and check each box when you can answer "yes" to the question.

☐ Does the beginning introduce the characters, context, and point of view?

☐ Does the body use a variety of techniques, such as transitional words and phrases, to sequence events so that they unfold naturally and logically?

☐ Does the conclusion follow from and reflect on the narrated experiences or events?

W.8.3b

Development of Ideas

Ask yourself the following questions. Then evaluate your narrative and check each box when you can answer "yes" to the question.

☐ Are the characters fully developed?

☐ Are they presented in an interesting, believable, and meaningful way?

☐ Do I use narrative techniques, such as dialogue, pacing, description, and reflection, to develop experiences, events, and/or characters?

Narrative

W.8.3b, d L.8.3 | Voice—Word Choice

Ask yourself the following questions. Then evaluate your narrative and check each box when you can answer "yes" to the question.

☐ Does my writing include precise words and phrases and relevant descriptive details to capture the action and convey the experiences and events?

☐ Does my story include descriptive, sensory language?

☐ Did I use knowledge of language and its conventions when writing?

L.8.1, c | Voice—Sentence Fluency

Ask yourself the following questions. Then evaluate your narrative and check each box when you can answer "yes" to the question.

☐ Do I demonstrate command of the conventions of standard English grammar and usage when writing?

☐ Do I form and use verbs in a variety of moods, such as indicative, imperative, interrogative, conditional, and subjunctive?

W.8.5 W.8.6 | Peer or Adult Review

Share your narrative and the checklists with a classmate or an adult. Have your reviewer use the checklists to evaluate your narrative and offer suggestions for improvement. Discuss the suggestions in person or e-mail specific questions or responses to their comments. Next, revise your story, as needed, possibly trying a new approach to cover areas of concern.

Edit and Proofread

L.8.1, c, d | # Correct Errors in Grammar

Editing involves correcting errors in grammar, usage, mechanics, and spelling. Begin the editing stage by taking a careful look at your sentences. Make sure that each sentence expresses a complete thought in a way that is grammatically correct. Use the checklist below to edit your sentences.

SENTENCE-EDITING CHECKLIST

☐ Have I avoided sentence fragments?

☐ Have I avoided run-on sentences?

☐ Do verbs agree with their subjects?

☐ Are pronouns used correctly?

☐ Are verbs used correctly?

☐ Have I avoided misplaced and dangling modifiers?

☐ Have I used phrases and clauses correctly?

☐ Have I used verb moods correctly?

L.8.2, c | # Correct Errors in Mechanics and Spelling

Next, check for and correct any errors in mechanics (punctuation and capitalization) and spelling. Use the checklist below to edit your story. You should also use a dictionary to check and confirm spellings.

PROOFREADING CHECKLIST

☐ Are commas and other punctuation marks used as needed?

☐ Are all words spelled correctly?

☐ Are capital letters used as needed?

W.8.5 W.8.6 | **Peer or Adult Review** Share your narrative and editing-and-proofreading checklists with a classmate or an adult. Have your reviewer use the checklists to evaluate your narrative and offer suggestions for improvement. Discuss the suggestions in person or e-mail specific questions or responses to the comments. Next, write the final draft of your narrative.

Narrative

Present/Publish

W.8.6 After you have written and polished your story, you will want to publish and present it. You may wish to consider some of these publishing and presenting options:

- Create a class anthology.
- Publish your story in an online forum or magazine.
- Enter your story into a writing contest.
- Perform your story as Readers Theater.

Consider using technology, including the Internet, to publish your story. By posting your narratives online, you and your classmates can read one another's stories and offer comments and feedback. You may wish to consult some of the projects in the Reading section of this book for additional publishing ideas that include technology.

Grammar Practice

L.8.1c Verb Moods

The mood of a verb refers to the manner in which a thought is expressed. The form of a verb used can vary, depending on its mood. There are three main verb moods: indicative, subjunctive (including conditional), and imperative.

Indicative Mood

The indicative is the most common mood used in English. A verb is in the indicative mood when it is part of a simple statement or question.

> **Example:** Toni Cade Bambara <u>wrote</u> "Raymond's Run."
> **Example:** It is about a girl who <u>runs</u> in a race.
> **Example:** You <u>will like</u> the story.

When an indicative verb is *interrogative* (part of a question), the subject and verb order is usually reversed, with the helping verb coming before the subject.

> **Example:** <u>Will</u> Squeaky <u>win</u> the race?
> **Example:** How good <u>will</u> Gretchen <u>be</u>?
> **Example:** Why <u>do</u> Squeaky and Gretchen <u>smile</u> at each other?

Subjunctive Mood

The subjunctive mood expresses an idea that is contrary to fact, is doubtful or uncertain, or is an assumption or a wish. One way the subjunctive verb form is used is in a *conditional* mood. A verb is said to be conditional when it is in a sentence that expresses uncertainty or how things might have been under certain conditions. The conditional mood often uses a verbal phrase containing *could, should, would,* or *might.*

> **Indicative:** If Squeaky <u>is</u> the winner, she will be glad.
> **Subjunctive:** If I <u>were</u> the winner, I <u>would</u> be glad.

> **Indicative:** If Gretchen <u>practices</u> hard, she may win.
> **Subjunctive:** If Gretchen <u>had practiced</u> more, she <u>might have won</u>.

The subjunctive is also used for suggestions, recommendations, commands, or expressions of urgency, when *could, should, would,* or *might* do not appear.

> **Indicative:** Squeaky made sure that her brother <u>watched</u> closely.
> **Subjunctive:** Squeaky suggested that her brother <u>watch</u> closely.

> **Indicative:** It is clear that Squeaky <u>is</u> confident in her ability.
> **Subjunctive:** It is important that Squeaky <u>be</u> confident in her ability.

> **Indicative:** People sometimes <u>teased</u> Squeaky's brother.
> **Subjunctive:** Squeaky demanded that people not <u>tease</u> her brother.

Narrative

Imperative Mood

A verb is in the imperative mood when it is part of a command or request. In an imperative sentence, the subject is always *you*. The word *you* may appear in the sentence, but it is usually just implied.

Example: <u>Read</u> the story.
Example: You <u>be</u> careful to notice the details.
Example: Please, <u>do</u> it now and <u>pay</u> attention.

EXERCISE: VERB MOODS

Fill in each blank with the correct form of the verb. The verb you should use is given in parentheses. Add any helping verbs you think you need.

1. Squeaky _____ (be) faster than most adults and all other children in her neighborhood.

2. However, if Squeaky's father races her, he _____ (beat) her every time.

3. Squeaky hinted that if Rosie made fun of Raymond, she _____ (make) Rosie sorry.

4. Squeaky says to Mr. Pearson, "_____ (write) my name down."

5. Before racing, Squeaky _____ (smell) the scent of apples.

6. If I _____ (be) Squeaky, would I be confident?

7. It is necessary that Squeaky _____ (run) a good race.

8. If Raymond became a runner, he _____ (be) a good one.

9. _____ (will) Gretchen _____ (help) Squeaky as Raymond's coach?

10. Squeaky and Gretchen _____ (smile) at each other after the race.

Check Your Writing Read through your short story to check your use of verbs. The verbs you find in the indicative mood—those in simple statements or questions—will probably not pose any difficulty for you. You should, however, pay special attention to any verbs that are in the subjunctive mood since this is a more complicated mood. Correct any inappropriate shifts in verb mood. Aim to use a variety of moods, as it will strengthen your writing and make it more interesting for the reader.

Narrative

Vocabulary

L.8.4, a, c L.8.6 Context as Clues to Meaning

In this lesson you will explore how a phrase, sentence, or paragraph can provide clues to a word's meaning. The other words and sentences around a word are called the word's **context.** Clues found in these surrounding words and sentences are called **context clues.**

Even when there are clear context clues that hint at a word's meaning, those clues may not tell you exactly what the word means. When you need to know the precise meaning of a word, consult a print or digital dictionary or glossary.

L.8.4, a Context Clues: Definitions

Sometimes context clues will tell you exactly what a word means by defining that word. To identify definition context clues, look for clues that tell the meaning of the unfamiliar word.

Example: The reasons for his behavior were <u>inexplicable</u>—no one could explain why he acted the way he did.

L.8.4, a, d L.8.5, b L.8.6 Context Clues: Word Relationships

One of the most common types of context clues is **synonyms,** or words that mean the same or almost the same thing. The example below suggests that *superfluous* and *unnecessary* are synonyms.

Example: I thought her umbrella was <u>superfluous</u> and mentioned that it seemed unnecessary on such a cloudless day.

Another type of common context clues is **antonyms,** or words that mean the opposite or nearly the opposite. The example below suggests that *sodden* means something very different from—maybe even the exact opposite of—*completely dry.*

Example: When the rain arrived, my clothes became <u>sodden</u> immediately, while hers remained completely dry!

To test the meaning of an unfamiliar word, try using your guess in the sentence in place of the word you don't know. If the sentence makes sense, your guess might be right. If it doesn't make sense, your guess is probably wrong.

Vocabulary

Exercise A: Using Word Relationships

Use context clues to guess the meaning of the underlined word. Circle the letter of the word's likely meaning. Remember to check your guess.

1. As he got older, his hair changed from thick to <u>sparse</u>.

    a. curly

    b. dyed

    c. well groomed

    d. thinly scattered

2. When I'm sad, having my dog nearby will often <u>console</u> me. Just having him around and loving me tends to soothe me.

    a. amuse

    b. comfort

    c. distract

    d. distress

3. She collected books steadily and never threw any away. Over the years, she <u>amassed</u> hundreds of them.

    a. read

    b. piled up

    c. arranged

    d. donated

4. What I had hoped would be <u>beneficial</u> was, instead, harmful. My efforts had just made things worse!

    a. helpful

    b. entertaining

    c. appropriate

    d. appreciated

5. He tried to explain as he saw the <u>perplexity</u> on my face, but the longer he talked, the deeper my bewilderment became.

    a. anger

    b. confusion

    c. exhaustion

    d. understanding

Vocabulary

Context Clues: Description and Contrast

L.8.4, a, d
L.8.6

Not all context clues that involve word relationships contain synonyms or antonyms. Sometimes more general clues are provided. A clue might be descriptive, which is similar to a synonym clue. A clue might also provide contrast, which is similar to an antonym clue.

Although the first example below contains no synonym for *annihilated*, you can tell by the description that it means something similar to "completely destroyed." In the second example, you can guess that tedious means "causing boredom."

> **Example:** My little brother <u>annihilated</u> my snow fort. He took a shovel and smashed it to pieces.

> **Example:** Painting the backyard fence was a <u>tedious</u> task. He could not remember ever being so bored.

In the first example below, a contrast to *callous* is provided. You can tell that *callous* means something similar to "insensitive." In the second example, a contrast to *inconvenient* is provided. You can tell that *inconvenient* probably means "not easy to do."

> **Example:** No, she's most definitely not <u>callous</u>. Instead, she feels everything very deeply and assumes that others will too.

> **Example:** He thought making the extra trip to the store would be <u>inconvenient</u>, but since he took his bicycle, it wound up being fast and easy.

Vocabulary

Exercise B: Using Context Clues: Description and Contrast
Use context clues to guess the meaning of the underlined word. Circle the
letter of the word's likely meaning. Remember to check your guess.

6. The light began to <u>dwindle</u>, so it became harder and harder to see what
everyone outside was doing.

    a. move   **c.** decrease

    b. change   **d.** end suddenly

7. I had hoped to spend the day relaxing, but I ended up with so many tasks
that the day was filled with <u>drudgery</u>.

    a. labor   **c.** idleness

    b. games   **d.** avoiding work

8. Make sure you have a good ladder and that it's positioned steadily.
Otherwise, you'll be sure to find yourself in a <u>precarious</u> situation.

    a. firm   **c.** insecure

    b. elevated   **d.** hopeless

9. Her smile and warm welcome indicated that Mrs. Asher was quite a
<u>genial</u> woman.

    a. wise   **c.** truthful

    b. careful   **d.** pleasant

10. The hero of the story <u>valiantly</u> pursued the men even though their threats
made everyone else too frightened to move.

    a. quickly   **c.** foolishly

    b. bravely   **d.** cheerfully

Vocabulary

L.8.4, a, d
L.8.5, b
L.8.6

Context Clues: Examples

Many times you can figure out what an unfamiliar word means by looking for examples provided by context clues. The examples given in the sentence below suggest that *din* is loud noise.

Example: The barking dog, hammering, and sirens all added to the <u>din</u>.

Exercise C: Using Examples

Use context clues to guess the meaning of the underlined word. Circle the letter of the word's likely meaning. Remember to check your guess.

11. Some of her <u>apparatus</u> consisted of hammers, nails, several saws, and measuring tape.

    a. work   **c.** equipment
    b. attempts   **d.** safety gear

12. My mom's car was completely smashed right after our house caught fire. It was a case of one <u>catastrophe</u> after another.

    a. disaster   **c.** surprise
    b. incident   **d.** small misfortune

13. I find it amazing that people <u>imperil</u> themselves by driving too fast and not wearing a seatbelt.

    a. excite   **c.** surprise
    b. endanger   **d.** involve

14. He always completed his homework neatly and on time, never caused trouble in class, and was helpful to the teacher and his classmates. His conduct was <u>irreproachable</u>.

    a. boring   **c.** blameless
    b. average   **d.** barely acceptable

15. Chairs, cars, and rocks are <u>inanimate</u> objects, unlike animals and people.

    a. simple   **c.** nonliving
    b. unnatural   **d.** uninteresting

Vocabulary

L.8.4, a, d
L.8.6

Context Clues: General Reasoning

Often you will find that a word's context clues don't fall into a particular category. You can still use your knowledge of words and language to get a good idea of an unfamiliar word's meaning.

For example: The basketball <u>ricocheted</u> off the backboard, and I grabbed it before it hit the floor.

Because the game of basketball and the function of a backboard are familiar to you, you would know that *ricocheted* means "bounced." Many times, context clues help you use what you do know to figure out what you don't know.

Exercise D: Using General Reasoning

Use context clues to guess the meaning of the underlined word. Circle the letter of the word's likely meaning. Remember to check your guess.

16. A bulldozer working on the street <u>obstructed</u> the cars attempting to travel there.

   a. helped   **c.** ruined
   b. blocked   **d.** annoyed

17. My grandfather's will left <u>bequests</u> of small amounts of money to each of his grandchildren.

   a. details   **c.** loans
   b. requests   **d.** inheritances

18. The gentle babbling of the <u>rill</u> that flowed outside the window lulled me to sleep.

   a. bird   **c.** brook
   b. lake   **d.** crickets

19. "Do it right this minute!" was the <u>directive</u> I received from my mother.

   a. request   **c.** comment
   b. command   **d.** suggestion

20. When he ran over my foot with his bike and did not apologize, I stared after him <u>indignantly</u>.

   a. rudely   **c.** angrily
   b. loudly   **d.** helplessly

Vocabulary

Word Parts as Clues to Meaning

In this lesson you will explore how word parts can be clues to meaning. First you will look at base words and roots, which are the most basic parts of words. Then you will look at affixes, such as prefixes and suffixes, which can slightly or significantly modify the meanings of roots and base words.

Base Words and Roots

L.8.4, b, c

Some words, such as *act*, have only one part. Other words, such as *inactive*, have several parts. *Inactive* contains a prefix at the beginning (*in-*) and a suffix at the end (*-ive*). All words, however, have a main part. If the main part is a complete word, as is the case with *act*, it's called a **base word**. For many words, however, the main part is not a whole word. For example, in the word *repopulate*, the main part of the word is *pop*. This is called a **root.**

Exercise A: Finding Base Words

Find the base word in each word and write it on the line.

1. misbehave _____

2. semicircle _____

3. preview _____

English words often contain roots from other languages, especially Greek and Latin. For this reason, and because roots are usually not whole words, roots can be harder to recognize than base words. It is important to learn the most common roots because a word's root holds the main meaning of the word. Anytime you learn the meaning of a root, it will help you understand words created from that root, which will be related in some way.

Here are some common roots found in English words:

Root	Meaning	Examples of Words
grat	pleasing	gratitude, ungrateful
ject	to throw	reject, inject
struct	to build	structure, destructive
vac	empty	vacuum, vacant
viv/vit	life	revive, vitamin

Vocabulary

Understanding the meanings of roots can help you figure out unfamiliar words because roots often give you a general sense of a word's meaning. However, the only way to be sure you have understood the precise meaning of an unfamiliar word is to check its meaning in a print or digital dictionary.

Exercise B: Identifying Roots
Find the root in each word and write it on the line.

4. vacancy _____

5. vital _____

6. projection _____

Exercise C: Using Roots to Determine Meaning
Use information in the chart on the previous page to answer the following questions. Circle the letter of the correct answer.

7. When people <u>evacuate</u> a building, they
   a. buy it.   b. move in.   c. go outside.

8. A person would probably be <u>gratified</u> to receive a
   a. shock.   b. compliment.   c. criticism.

9. If you think that a review of your work is <u>constructive</u>, you think it
   a. helps you.   b. insults you.   c. is useless.

10. When someone <u>interjects</u> a comment into a discussion, that is similar to
    a. a joke.   b. a disagreement.   c. an interruption.

11. Someone who is known for being <u>vivacious</u> is
    a. lively.   b. competitive.   c. dangerous.

Vocabulary

L.8.4, b, c **Prefixes**

A **prefix** is a word part that is placed before the base word or root to modify its meaning. Sometimes the meaning changes slightly. For example, the meaning of *reset* is similar to the meaning of *set*. The *re-* prefix simply adds the idea of "again." In other cases, a prefix can completely change a base word's or root's meaning. For example, the meanings of *approve* and *disapprove* are opposite.

Exercise D: Identifying Prefixes

Find the prefix in each word and write it on the line.

12. biweekly _____

13. international _____

14. impossible _____

Here are some common prefixes found in English words:

Prefix	Meaning	Examples of Words
mal-	bad or wrong	malnutrition, malfunction
ex-	out	export, exhale
re-	again	review, rebuild
re-	back	return, reflect
post-	after or later	postscript, postpone

Some prefixes, such as *re-*, have more than one meaning. For example, *ex-* can mean "former" instead of "out." However, knowing a particular meaning of a prefix can still be a useful clue to the word's meaning.

No matter how helpful a clue is, though, it is still only a clue. The only way to be sure you have understood the precise meaning of an unfamiliar word is to check its meaning in a print or digital dictionary.

Vocabulary

Exercise E: Using Prefixes to Determine Meaning

Use information in the chart on the previous page and your knowledge of base words and roots to answer the following questions. Circle the letter of the correct answer.

15. Someone who calls a person a <u>malcontent</u> is saying that the person has a

   a. bad attitude.   **b.** good idea.   **c.** sense of humor.

16. If you feel <u>revitalized</u>, you are feeling

   a. content.   **b.** energetic.   **c.** threatened.

17. People usually receive <u>postoperative</u> care in a

   a. kitchen.   **b.** beauty salon.   **c.** hospital.

18. If you <u>exclaim</u> something, you are

   a. whispering it.   **b.** saying it out loud.   **c.** thinking it.

19. People would tend to <u>recoil</u> from something that they thought was

   a. funny.   **b.** attractive.   **c.** disgusting.

Vocabulary

L.8.4, b, c | ## Suffixes

A **suffix** is a word part added to the end of a root or base word that modifies its meaning in some way. The most common use of suffixes is to change the tense or part of speech of a word—for example, to change *jump* into *jumped* or the noun *fever* into the adjective *feverish*. In a few cases, a suffix changes a word's meaning more significantly, such as when *aim* becomes *aimless*.

Adding suffixes often involves slight adjustments to spelling. For example, the final *e* drops off when *bone* becomes *bony*; a final consonant is doubled when *star* becomes *starring*; final *y*'s may change to *i*'s or even drop off.

You can often tell that a word contains a suffix because the suffix is familiar or because the whole word contains a familiar base word or root.

Exercise F: Identifying Suffixes
Find the suffix in each word and write it on the line.

20. friendly _____

21. treatment _____

22. changeable _____

Here are some common suffixes found in English words:

Suffix	Meaning	Examples of Words
-al	having to do with	logical, natural
-ary	like, connected with	honorary, momentary
-etic/-ic	relating to	alphabetic, dramatic
-ify	to make	beautify, mystify
-ile	having to do with	percentile, projectile

Knowing the meanings of common suffixes can be helpful when you come across an unfamiliar word. Sometimes the suffix will help you guess the meaning of the word. However, the only way to be sure that your guess is correct is to check the meaning in a print or digital dictionary.

Vocabulary

Exercise G: Using Suffixes to Determine Meaning

Use information in the chart on the previous page and your knowledge of base words and roots to answer the following questions. Circle the letter of the correct answer.

23. If you go to <u>rehearsal</u>, you are going somewhere to

    a. sleep.   **b.** practice.   **c.** argue.

24. A <u>cautionary</u> speech is one that contains a

    a. story.   **b.** joke.   **c.** warning.

25. If you want to <u>diversify</u> your goals, you want them to be

    a. more varied.   **b.** more popular.   **c.** easier to reach.

26. Doing something <u>strategic</u> always involves

    a. kindness.   **b.** skillful planning.   **c.** muscular strength.

27. Someone whose behavior is <u>infantile</u> is acting like a

    a. bully.   **b.** parent.   **c.** baby.

Vocabu

Denotation, Connotation, and Shades of Meaning

Denotation and Connotation

Not only does the English language have many words, but most words have several meanings. The **denotations** of a word are the meanings found in the dictionary. Some words have associated meanings, called **connotations**.

The connotation of a word is the ideas or feelings associated with that word that are not part of its definition. For example, one definition of *rare* is "seldom occurring or found," but *rare* calls to mind value and desirability that is not present in the word *uncommon*. Likewise, *soggy* suggests an unpleasant condition—an association not linked to the word *moist*.

A word's connotation can be neutral, positive, or negative. For example, the word *competition* has a neutral connotation, whereas *rivalry* has a more negative connotation.

Connotation can be powerful. Because people react emotionally to certain words, writers carefully choose their words to create specific feelings in readers. For example, the color of a green sweater might be described in a catalog as "moss," not "mold." *Moss* has a neutral or positive connotation, whereas *mold* has a negative connotation.

Exercise A: Recognizing Connotation

For each pair of synonyms, select the one word that has the more positive connotation and the one that has the more negative connotation. Write each word in the appropriate column.

		Positive	Negative
1.	strange/quaint	_____	_____
2.	curious/nosy	_____	_____
3.	determined/stubborn	_____	_____
4.	childish/childlike	_____	_____
5.	relaxed/idle	_____	_____

L.8.4c
L.8.5, c

Shades of Meaning

In addition to connotative differences, synonyms can have denotative differences, because synonyms rarely mean exactly the same thing. For example, the meanings of *smell* and *stink* are different, even though they are synonyms. A stink is not just a smell; it's an extremely bad smell. Similarly, *to ridicule* is different from *to disapprove*. *Ridicule* contains a sense of scorn that *disapprove* does not. These differences among synonyms are called **shades of meaning.**

It is important to consider shades of meaning when you read and when you write. Although a thesaurus, which provides synonyms for words, is a valuable tool, it should be used with care. Only a dictionary can provide the precise meaning of a word. When you are unsure of exactly what a word means, you should consult a print or digital dictionary.

Exercise B: Recognizing Shades of Meaning

Answer the following questions on the lines provided. You may use a dictionary if you are unsure of the answer.

6. How is <u>uproar</u> different from <u>noise</u>? _____

_____

7. How is a <u>disaster</u> different from a <u>problem</u>? _____

_____

8. How is <u>conceit</u> different from <u>pride</u>? _____

_____

9. How is <u>to toss</u> different from <u>to throw</u>? _____

_____

10. How is a <u>friend</u> different from an <u>acquaintance</u>? _____

_____

Vocabulary

Grade 8 Common Core State Standards

Grade 8 Common Core State Standards

Reading Standards for Literature

Key Ideas and Details

1. Cite the textual evidence that most strongly supports an analysis of what the text says explicitly as well as inferences drawn from the text.

2. Determine a theme or central idea of a text and analyze its development over the course of the text, including its relationship to the characters, setting, and plot; provide an objective summary of the text.

3. Analyze how particular lines of dialogue or incidents in a story or drama propel the action, reveal aspects of a character, or provoke a decision.

Craft and Structure

4. Determine the meaning of words and phrases as they are used in a text, including figurative and connotative meanings; analyze the impact of specific word choices on meaning and tone, including analogies or allusions to other texts.

5. Compare and contrast the structure of two or more texts and analyze how the differing structure of each text contributes to its meaning and style.

6. Analyze how differences in the points of view of the characters and the audience or reader (e.g., created through the use of dramatic irony) create such effects as suspense or humor.

Integration of Knowledge and Ideas

7. Analyze the extent to which a filmed or live production of a story or drama stays faithful to or departs from the text or script, evaluating the choices made by the director or actors.

8. (Not applicable to literature)

9. Analyze how a modern work of fiction draws on themes, patterns of events, or character types from myths, traditional stories, or religious works such as the Bible, including describing how the material is rendered new.

Range of Reading and Level of Text Complexity

10. By the end of the year, read and comprehend literature, including stories, dramas, and poems, at the high end of grades 6–8 text complexity band independently and proficiently.

Reading Standards for Informational Text

Key Ideas and Details

1. Cite the textual evidence that most strongly supports an analysis of what the text says explicitly as well as inferences drawn from the text.

2. Determine a central idea of a text and analyze its development over the course of the text, including its relationship to supporting ideas; provide an objective summary of the text.

3. Analyze how a text makes connections among and distinctions between individuals, ideas, or events (e.g., through comparisons, analogies, or categories).

Craft and Structure

4. Determine the meaning of words and phrases as they are used in a text, including figurative, connotative, and technical meanings; analyze the impact of specific word choices on meaning and tone, including analogies or allusions to other texts.

5. Analyze in detail the structure of a specific paragraph in a text, including the role of particular sentences in developing and refining a key concept.

6. Determine an author's point of view or purpose in a text and analyze how the author acknowledges and responds to conflicting evidence or viewpoints.

Integration of Knowledge and Ideas

7. Evaluate the advantages and disadvantages of using different mediums (e.g., print or digital text, video, multimedia) to present a particular topic or idea.

8. Delineate and evaluate the argument and specific claims in a text, assessing whether the reasoning is sound and the evidence is relevant and sufficient; recognize when irrelevant evidence is introduced.

9. Analyze a case in which two or more texts provide conflicting information on the same topic and identify where the texts disagree on matters of fact or interpretation.

Range of Reading and Level of Text Complexity

10. By the end of the year, read and comprehend literary nonfiction at the high end of the grades 6–8 text complexity band independently and proficiently.

Writing Standards

Text Types and Purposes

1. Write arguments to support claims with clear reasons and relevant evidence.

   a. Introduce claim(s), acknowledge and distinguish the claim(s) from alternate or opposing claims, and organize the reasons and evidence logically.

   b. Support claim(s) with logical reasoning and relevant evidence, using accurate, credible sources and demonstrating an understanding of the topic or text.

   c. Use words, phrases, and clauses to create cohesion and clarify the relationships among claim(s), counterclaims, reasons, and evidence.

   d. Establish and maintain a formal style.

   e. Provide a concluding statement or section that follows from and supports the argument presented.

2. Write informative/explanatory texts to examine a topic and convey ideas, concepts, and information through the selection, organization, and analysis of relevant content.

   a. Introduce a topic clearly, previewing what is to follow; organize ideas, concepts, and information into broader categories; include formatting (e.g., headings), graphics (e.g., charts, tables), and multimedia when useful to aiding comprehension.

   b. Develop the topic with relevant, well-chosen facts, definitions, concrete details, quotations, or other information and examples.

   c. Use appropriate and varied transitions to create cohesion and clarify the relationships among ideas and concepts.

   d. Use precise language and domain-specific vocabulary to inform about or explain the topic.

   e. Establish and maintain a formal style.

   f. Provide a concluding statement or section that follows from and supports the information or explanation presented.

3. Write narratives to develop real or imagined experiences or events using effective technique, relevant descriptive details, and well-structured event sequences.

   a. Engage and orient the reader by establishing a context and point of view and introducing a narrator and/or characters; organize an event sequence that unfolds naturally and logically.

b. Use narrative techniques, such as dialogue, pacing, description, and reflection, to develop experiences, events, and/or characters.

c. Use a variety of transition words, phrases, and clauses to convey sequence, signal shifts from one time frame or setting to another, and show the relationships among experiences and events.

d. Use precise words and phrases, relevant descriptive details, and sensory language to capture the action and convey experiences and events.

e. Provide a conclusion that follows from and reflects on the narrated experiences or events.

Production and Distribution of Writing

4. Produce clear and coherent writing in which the development, organization, and style are appropriate to task, purpose, and audience. (Grade-specific expectations for writing types are defined in standards 1–3 above.)

5. With some guidance and support from peers and adults, develop and strengthen writing as needed by planning, revising, editing, rewriting, or trying a new approach, focusing on how well purpose and audience have been addressed. (Editing for conventions should demonstrate command of Language standards 1–3 up to and including grade 8.)

6. Use technology, including the Internet, to produce and publish writing and present the relationships between information and ideas efficiently as well as to interact and collaborate with others.

Research to Build and Present Knowledge

7. Conduct short research projects to answer a question (including a self-generated question), drawing on several sources and generating additional related, focused questions that allow for multiple avenues of exploration.

8. Gather relevant information from multiple print and digital sources, using search terms effectively; assess the credibility and accuracy of each source; and quote or paraphrase the data and conclusions of others while avoiding plagiarism and following a standard format for citation.

9. Draw evidence from literary or informational texts to support analysis, reflection, and research.

a. Apply *grade 8 Reading standards* to literature (e.g., "Analyze how a modern work of fiction draws on themes, patterns of events, or character types from myths, traditional stories, or religious works such as the Bible, including describing how the material is rendered new").

b. Apply *grade 8 Reading standards* to literary nonfiction (e.g., "Delineate and evaluate the argument and specific claims in a text, assessing whether the reasoning is sound and the evidence is relevant and sufficient; recognize when irrelevant evidence is introduced").

Range of Writing

10. Write routinely over extended time frames (time for research, reflection, and revision) and shorter time frames (a single sitting or a day or two) for a range of discipline-specific tasks, purposes, and audiences.

Speaking and Listening Standards

Comprehension and Collaboration

1. Engage effectively in a range of collaborative discussions (one-on-one, in groups, and teacherled) with diverse partners on *grade 8 topics*, *texts, and issues*, building on others' ideas and expressing their own clearly.

a. Come to discussions prepared, having read or researched material under study; explicitly draw on that preparation by referring to evidence on the topic, text, or issue to probe and reflect on ideas under discussion.

b. Follow rules for collegial discussions and decision-making, track progress toward specific goals and deadlines, and define individual roles as needed.

c. Pose questions that connect the ideas of several speakers and respond to others' questions and comments with relevant evidence, observations, and ideas.

d. Acknowledge new information expressed by others, and, when warranted, qualify or justify their own views in light of the evidence presented.

2. Analyze the purpose of information presented in diverse media and formats (e.g., visually, quantitatively, orally) and evaluate the motives (e.g., social, commercial, political) behind its presentation.

3. Delineate a speaker's argument and specific claims, evaluating the soundness of the reasoning and relevance and sufficiency of the evidence and identifying when irrelevant evidence is introduced.

Presentation of Knowledge and Ideas

4. Present claims and findings, emphasizing salient points in a focused, coherent manner with relevant evidence, sound valid reasoning, and well-chosen details; use appropriate eye contact, adequate volume, and clear pronunciation.

5. Integrate multimedia and visual displays into presentations to clarify information, strengthen claims and evidence, and add interest.

6. Adapt speech to a variety of contexts and tasks, demonstrating command of formal English when indicated or appropriate. (See grade 8 Language standards 1 and 3 for specific expectations.)

Language Standards

Conventions of Standard English

1. Demonstrate command of the conventions of standard English grammar and usage when writing or speaking.

   a. Explain the function of verbals (gerunds, participles, infinitives) in general and their function in particular sentences.

   b. Form and use verbs in the active and passive voice.

   c. Form and use verbs in the indicative, imperative, interrogative, conditional, and subjunctive mood.

   d. Recognize and correct inappropriate shifts in verb voice and mood.

2. Demonstrate command of the conventions of standard English capitalization, punctuation, and spelling when writing.

   a. Use punctuation (comma, ellipsis, dash) to indicate a pause or break.

   b. Use an ellipsis to indicate an omission.

   c. Spell correctly.

Knowledge of Language

3. Use knowledge of language and its conventions when writing, speaking, reading, or listening.

   a. Use verbs in the active and passive voice and in the conditional and subjunctive mood to achieve particular effects (e.g., emphasizing the actor or the action; expressing uncertainty or describing a state contrary to fact).

Vocabulary Acquisition and Use

4. Determine or clarify the meaning of unknown and multiple-meaning words or phrases based on *grade 8 reading and content*, choosing flexibly from a range of strategies.

   a. Use context (e.g., the overall meaning of a sentence or paragraph; a word's position or function in a sentence) as a clue to the meaning of a word or phrase.

b. Use common, grade-appropriate Greek or Latin affixes and roots as clues to the meaning of a word (e.g., *precede*, *recede*, *secede*).

c. Consult general and specialized reference materials (e.g., dictionaries, glossaries, thesauruses), both print and digital, to find the pronunciation of a word or determine or clarify its precise meaning or its part of speech.

d. Verify the preliminary determination of the meaning of a word or phrase (e.g., by checking the inferred meaning in context or in a dictionary).

5. Demonstrate understanding of figurative language, word relationships, and nuances in word meanings.

a. Interpret figures of speech (e.g. verbal irony, puns) in context.

b. Use the relationship between particular words to better understand each of the words.

c. Distinguish among the connotations (associations) of words with similar denotations (definitions) (e.g., *bullheaded*, *willful*, *firm*, *persistent*, *resolute*).

6. Acquire and use accurately grade-appropriate general academic and domain-specific words and phrases; gather vocabulary knowledge when considering a word or phrase important to comprehension or expression.